W9-CCD-555

SPANISH GRAMMAR

Juan Kattán-Ibarra

TEACH YOURSELF BOOKS

Long-renowned as the authoritative source for self-guided learning – with more than 30 million copies sold worldwide – the *Teach Yourself* series includes over 200 titles in the fields of languages, crafts, hobbies, sports, and other leisure activities.

Library of Congress Catalog Card Number: 92-80864

First published in UK 1991 by Hodder Headline Plc, 338 Euston Road, London NW1 3BH

First published in US 1992 by NTC Publishing Group, 4255 West Touhy Avenue, Lincolnwood (Chicago), Illinois 60646 – 1975 U.S.A.

Typeset by Cotswold Typesetting Ltd, Gloucester
Printed in Great Britain by Cox & Wyman Ltd, Reading, Berkshire.

Impression number	16	15	14	13	12	11	10	9
Year		1999	1998	1997	1996	1995		

Contents

Introduction

This book is designed as a reference guide for those who, with or without the help of a teacher, need to study all the essentials of Spanish grammar. A particular feature of the book is its two-fold approach to the language, from a communicative perspective as well as from a traditionally grammatical point of view.

In terms of communication, this reference guide covers all the basic language functions or uses, such as asking and giving personal information (Unit 1), expressing location (Unit 5), asking and giving opinions (Unit 14) and giving directions and instructions (Unit 20). Each one of these basic language functions – making up 23 graded Units in all – leads into the constructions and forms which are needed to express them. Thus, and without losing sight of language usage, all the essentials of Spanish grammar are covered, including nouns, adjectives, adverbs, pronouns as well as simple and compound tenses. Important points not covered within the Units are treated separately in the section **Apuntes gramaticales** (*Grammar notes*).

On the contents page, each Unit lists both language uses and grammatical terms. This allows you to approach the book from either perspective. If you want to look up particular grammar points you should consult the index at the back of the book.

How to use this book

The following procedure is suggested for working through each Unit: read the list of **Objetivos** (*objectives*), which give information about the language uses or functions that are studied in the Unit. Then read the **Contenido gramatical** (*grammatical contents*) which lists all the constructions and forms associated with the language functions included under **Objetivos**. You can then go onto the **Nota preliminar** (*preliminary note*) which contains brief and simple explanations of the type of language you are going to encounter in the rest of the Unit. The associations between Spanish and English made in this section and the bilingual examples illustrating each use of the language are there to help you ease your way into the **Resumen gramatical** (*grammar summary*). Here you will find detailed explanations of some of the points included in the **Contenido gramatical**. Read this section carefully and study the examples and their English translation, then try writing further examples of your own. Occasionally it may be useful to go back to the sentences under **Nota preliminar** to see the link between a certain language usage and a particular grammar point.

Language always functions within a context, so the purpose of the section **En contexto** (*in context*) is to show you how the language you have studied in the Unit can be used. Read the dialogues and other passages – extracts from letters, notes, etc. – paying particular attention to those points highlighted in the **Nota preliminar** and **Resumen gramatical**. New words are listed after each text and any points requiring explanation are dealt with under **Explicaciones**. If you feel you need further practice, use the dialogues and other passages as a model to write new ones.

Once you feel confident that you have understood and are able to handle the new language taught in the Unit, you may want to go a step further into the **Expansión** (*expansion*). This, as the name implies, is intended as an expansion of the grammar and language functions already covered in the previous sections. Most of the points included here are less frequent alternative forms of expression for the language uses listed under **Objetivos**. Some secondary uses of language are also covered in this section.

All words used throughout the book – whether in sentences, dialogues or other texts – are listed in the Spanish–English vocabulary at the end of the book.

1 Asking and giving personal information

Objetivos

In this Unit you will learn how to:

Say who you are • State your nationality • Say where you are from • Say what your occupation is • Give similar information about other people • Ask personal information about other people

Contenido gramatical

Subject pronouns • 'Ser' in the present tense • Gender of nouns • Plural of nouns • Adjectives indicating nationality • Interrogative sentences • Negative sentences

Nota preliminar

To ask and give personal information you will need the Spanish equivalent of words like *I, you, he, she,* etc., which are called subject pronouns. You will also need a verb, in this case the verb **ser**, which means *to be*. Have a look at these examples and their English translation before going onto the **Resumen gramatical**.

Saying who you are

Soy Antonio García	*I'm Antonio García*
Soy Ana Hidalgo	*I'm Ana Hidalgo*

Stating your nationality

Soy español   *I'm Spanish* (masc.)
Soy española   *I'm Spanish* (fem.)

Saying where you are from

Soy de Madrid   *I'm from Madrid*
Soy de Salamanca   *I'm from Salamanca*

Saying what your occupation is

Soy arquitecto   *I'm an architect*
Soy estudiante   *I'm a student*

Giving similar information about other people

Él es Roberto Pérez   *He's Roberto Pérez*
Es chileno   *He's Chilean*
Es de Santiago   *He's from Santiago*
Es profesor   *He's a teacher*

Asking personal information about other people

Formally:
¿Es usted española?   *Are you Spanish?*
¿Es usted de Madrid?   *Are you from Madrid?*
¿Es usted secretaria?   *Are you a secretary?*

Informally:
¿Eres argentino?   *Are you Argentinian?*
¿Eres de Buenos Aires?   *Are you from Buenos Aires?*
¿Eres estudiante?   *Are you a student?*

Resumen gramatical

1 Subject pronouns

To say *I*, *you*, *he*, *she*, etc. in Spanish, we use the following set of words:

	Singular
yo	*I*
tú	*you* (familiar)
usted	*you* (polite)
él	*he*
ella	*she*
	Plural
nosotros/as	*we* (masc./fem.)
vosotros/as	*you* (familiar, masc./fem.)
ustedes	*you* (polite)
ellos	*they* (masc.)
ellas	*they* (fem.)

Familiar and polite forms of address

Notice that Spanish uses familiar and polite forms of address. The familiar forms (**tú** and **vosotros**) are used very extensively in Spain today, even among people who have never met before. However, in business and official situations, it may generally be safer to use the polite form to start with and then wait and see what the other person is using and do likewise. In writing, **usted** and **ustedes** are normally found in abbreviated form as **Vd.** and **Vds.**

Latin American usage

Latin Americans do not use the familiar plural **vosotros**. Instead, they will use **ustedes**, without differentiating between familiarity and formality. Consequently, the verb forms used to address a group of people will be those corresponding to **ustedes**. In the singular, the distinction between **tú** and **usted** still remains. In abbreviated form, in Latin America, **usted** and **ustedes** become **Ud.** and **Uds.**

Omission of subject pronouns

Generally, subject pronouns are omitted in Spanish, except at the start of a conversation, to emphasise or to avoid ambiguity, as with **él**, **ella, usted** (and their plural equivalents) which always share the same verb forms.

Él es español	*He's Spanish*
Ella es española	*She's Spanish*
Usted es español	*You're Spanish*

2   *Ser* (to be) in the present tense

Ser is the verb most frequently used in Spanish when giving basic personal information such as your name, nationality, place of origin and occupation. Here is **ser** fully conjugated in the present tense:

	Singular
yo soy	*I am*
tú eres	*you are* (familiar)
usted es	*you are* (polite)
él, ella es	*he, she is*
	Plural
nosotros somos	*we are*
vosotros sois	*you are* (familiar)
ustedes son	*you are* (polite)
ellos, ellas son	*they are* (masc./fem.)

Nota: for other uses of **ser** see Units 2, 3, 5, 6, 11, and pages 227–228 of **Apuntes gramaticales** (*Grammar notes*).

3 Gender of nouns

Masculine or feminine?

All nouns in Spanish are either masculine or feminine. Nouns which refer to people, such as those indicating professions or occupations, will normally agree in gender with the person referred to. The following simple rules will help you to form the feminine of nouns denoting professions:

- Change the -o to -a.

    Él es abogado   *He's a lawyer*
    Ella es abogada   *She's a lawyer*

- Add -a to the consonant.

    Juan es profesor   *Juan is a teacher*
    María es profesora   *María is a teacher*

- Nouns which end in -e do not normally change for masculine and feminine.

    Pedro es estudiante   *Pedro is a student*
    Carmen es estudiante *Carmen is a student*

But there are exceptions:

    Él es dependiente   *He's a shop assistant*
    Ella es dependienta   *She's a shop assistant*
    Él es jefe de ventas   *He's a sales manager*
    Ella es jefa de ventas   *She's a sales manager*

- Nouns which end in -ista never change for masculine and feminine.

    Él es dentista   *He's a dentist*
    Ella es dentista *She's a dentist*

Nota: With certain professions, you may still hear the masculine form used with reference to women, for example:

Él es médico	*He's a doctor*
Ella es médico	*She's a doctor*

However, new attitudes towards women in Spanish society are bringing about changes in this area of language usage.

Nota: There is more on the gender of nouns in Unit 2 and on pages 215–216 of **Apuntes gramaticales** (*Grammar notes*).

4 Plural of nouns

As in English, nouns in Spanish can have singular and plural forms. The plural of nouns is normally formed by adding -s to the singular form, unless the word ends in a consonant, in which case you add -es.

Él es arquitecto	*He's an architect*
Ellos son arquitectos	*They're architects*
Soy doctor	*I'm a doctor*
Somos doctores	*We're doctors*

Nota: See also pages 216–217 of **Apuntes gramaticales**.

5 Adjectives indicating nationality

Masculine or feminine?
Adjectives of nationality, like many adjectives in Spanish, have masculine and feminine forms. To form the feminine from a masculine noun of nationality or origin change -o to -a or add -a to the consonant, as in:

John es británico	*John is British*
Sarah es británica	*Sarah is British*
Peter es inglés	*Peter is English*
Ann es inglesa	*Ann is English*

Singular and plural

The plural of adjectives, like that of nouns, is normally formed by adding -s to the singular form, unless the word ends in a consonant, in which case you add -es.

John es británico	*John is British*
John y Sarah son británicos	*John and Sarah are British*
Peter es inglés	*Peter is English*
Peter y Ann son ingleses	*Peter and Ann are English*

Notice that when the adjective refers to both male and female we use the masculine form.

Adjectives which end in -i and -ú add -es to form the plural.

Él es paquistaní	*He's Pakistani*
Ellos son paquistaníes	*They're Pakistani*
Ella es hindú	*She's Indian*
Ellas son hindúes	*They're Indian*

Adjectives which end in -z change -z into -c and add -es.

Paco es andaluz	*Paco is Andalusian*
Paco y Antonio son anda-	*Paco and Antonio are Anda-*
luces	*lusian*

6 Interrogative sentences

It is possible to form questions in Spanish in several ways:

• Using the same word order as in a statement, but with a rising intonation.

¿Usted es española?	*Are you Spanish?*

• Reversing the order subject-verb.

¿Es usted irlandés?	*Are you Irish?*

• Using either ¿**verdad**? (literally, *true*) or ¿**no**? attached to the statement.

> Usted es escocés, ¿**verdad**?   *You're Scottish, aren't you?*
> Ella es americana, ¿**no**?   *She's American isn't she?*

7   Negative sentences

Negative sentences are formed simply by using the word **no** before the verb.

> ¿**No** es usted español?   *Aren't you Spanish?*
> No, **no** soy español   *No, I'm not Spanish*

Notice the double negative, as in English, in the second sentence.

En contexto

1   *Study these conversations between people who have just met and are getting to know each other. The first exchange is formal and the second one informal.*

(a) **Señor**   ¿Es Vd. española?
   Señora   Sí, soy española, ¿y Vd.?
   Señor   Soy mexicano. Soy de Guadalajara.
   Señora   Yo soy de Madrid.

sí	*yes*
y	*and*
de	*from*

(b) **Carlos**   Hola. ¿Cómo te llamas?
   Carmen   Me llamo Carmen, ¿y tú?

Carlos	Yo soy Carlos López. ¿Eres de Madrid?
Carmen	No, no soy de Madrid. Soy de Salamanca.

hola	*hello*
¿cómo te llamas?	*what's your name?* (fam.)

2   *Look at this piece of writing which gives personal information.*

...ne llamo Alfonso González, soy español, de Sevilla. Soy estudiante de medicina ...

Explicaciones

1   *Asking someone's name and saying your name*

To ask someone's name in a formal way use the phrase

¿Cómo se llama Vd.?   *What's your name?* (literally, *what are you called?*).

The reply, as in dialogue (*b*) above will be

Me llamo	*My name is* (literally, *I'm called*), or
Soy	*I am*

2   *Saying what your occupation is*

When giving your occupation or profession Spanish does not use the equivalent of the English word *a*, as in *I'm a student*.

Soy estudiante   *I'm a student*
Es arquitecto   *He's an architect*

Expansión

1   Asking and giving information about status or rank, religion and political affiliation

Information such as the above may also be asked and given with the verb **ser**.

Soy director gerente   *I'm a managing director*
Es general   *He's a general*
¿**Eres** católico?   *Are you a catholic?*
Él **es** socialista   *He's a socialist*

Notice the omission of the equivalent of English '*a*' in ¿**Eres católico?**, **Él es socialista.**

2   Asking and giving information about marital status

To ask and give information about marital status we may use the verb **ser**, as in

¿**Es** usted casado o soltero?   *Are you married or single?*
Soy casado   *I'm married*

More frequently, however, this information is asked and given with the verb **estar**, also meaning *to be*, which is normally used when referring to states or conditions, such as the state of being single or married.

¿**Está** usted casado o soltero?   *Are you married or single?*
Estoy soltero   *I'm single*

For the full forms of **estar** see Unit 3.

2   Identifying people, places and things

Objetivos

In this Unit you will learn how to:

Introduce people • Greet people when being introduced • Identify people, places and things • Ask questions in order to identify people, places and things

Contenido gramatical

Demonstrative adjectives and pronouns • 'Ser' in introductions and identification • Definite articles • Interrogative words '¿quién?', '¿cuál?', '¿qué?' • Possessive adjective 'mi'

Nota preliminar

To identify or introduce people you will need the Spanish equivalent of words like *this*, *that*, *these* and *those*, followed by the singular or plural form of **ser** (*to be*) plus a proper name or a phrase such as **mi marido** (*my husband*), **mis hijos** (*my children*). For example

Éste es Antonio	*This is Antonio*
Éste es mi marido	*This is my husband*
Éstos son mis hijos	*These are my children*

The same construction may be used to identify places and things, as in **ésta es Sevilla** (*this is Seville*), **ése es mi coche** (*that is my car*).

Questions to elicit identification such as *who's that gentleman?*, *which is the house?*, *what is this?*, will require the use of interrogative words like **¿quién?** (*who?*), **¿cuál?** (*which?*, *what?*), **¿qué?** (what?): **¿quién es ese señor?**, **¿cuál es la casa?**, **¿qué es esto?**

Have a look at these examples and their English translation before going on to the **Resumen gramatical**.

Introducing people

Ésta es Carmen	*This is Carmen*
Ésta es mi mujer	*This is my wife*
Éste es mi hermano Raúl	*This is my brother Raul*

Greeting people when being introduced

Encantado/a*	*Pleased to meet you*
Mucho gusto	*Pleased to meet you*
Hola	*Hello*

Identifying people, places and things

Ése es el señor García	*That's señor García*
Éste es mi pueblo	*This is my town*
Aquéllas son mis llaves	*Those are my keys*

Ask questions leading to the identification of people, places and things

¿Quién es esa chica?	*Who's that girl?*
¿Cuál es el museo?	*Which is the museum?*
¿Cuál es la llave?	*Which is the key?*

* For an explanation of **encantado/a** see **Explicaciones** on page 19.

Resumen gramatical

1 Demonstrative adjectives and pronouns

Look at the examples above once again and study the Spanish equivalent of *this, these* and *that, those*. Unlike English, which only distinguishes between singular and plural, Spanish also makes a distinction between masculine and feminine.

Forms of demonstratives

This, these (next to you)

este señor (masc.)	*this gentleman*
esta señora (fem.)	*this lady*
estos señores (masc.)	*these gentlemen*
estas señoras (fem.)	*these ladies*

That, those (near you)

ese hotel (masc.)	*that hotel*
esa habitación (fem.)	*that room*
esos hoteles (masc.)	*those hotels*
esas habitaciones (fem.)	*those rooms*

Spanish also differs from English in having a separate set of words to identify or point at someone or something which is far from you. In English, however, the translation would still be *that, those*.

That, those (far from you)

aquel chico (masc.)	*that boy*
aquella chica (fem.)	*that girl*
aquellos chicos (masc.)	*those boys*
aquellas chicas (fem.)	*those girls*

Adjectives and pronouns

In all the examples above, the demonstratives have been followed by nouns (e.g. **este señor, ese hotel, aquel chico**), in which case words such as **este, ese, aquel** are functioning as adjectives. But they may also be used to refer to a noun without mentioning it specifically, for example **éste** (*this one*), **ése** (*that one*), **aquél** (*that one*). In this case, they act as pronouns, and they are normally written with an accent, to distinguish them from the adjectives. However, the **Real Academia Española** (*The Spanish Royal Academy*) has ruled that the omission of the accent is perfectly correct except when there is ambiguity (which rarely arises). Nevertheless, most educated people in the Hispanic world continue to use the accent.

Neuter demonstratives

Neuter forms are used when we are not referring to a specific noun, as in:

¿Qué es **esto**?	*What's this?*
¿Qué es **eso**?	*What's that?*
¿Qué es **aquello**?	*What's that?*

2   *Ser* in introductions and identification

In the examples under **Nota preliminar**, notice the use of **ser** – **es** for singular and **son** for plural – for identifying people, places and things:

Ése es el señor García	*That is Mr. García*
Éste es mi pueblo	*This is my town*
Aquéllas son mis llaves	*Those are my keys*

If we are introducing or identifying ourselves we need to use **soy** in the singular and **somos** in the plural, for example

Soy Paco Martínez	*I'm Paco Martínez*
Somos los señores García	*We're the Garcías*

Notice also the use of **ser** when enquiring about someone or something:

¿Quién **es** esa señorita?   *Who's that young lady?*
¿Cuál **es** el coche?   *Which is the car?*

Nota: For the full forms of **ser** see Unit 1.

3 Definite articles (*the*)

Look at the use of the definite article (*the*) in these sentences:

¿Cuál es **el** hotel?   *Which is the hotel?*
¿Cuál **es la** habitación?   *Which is the room?*
Éstos son **los** pasaportes   *These are the passports*
Éstas son **las** llaves   *These are the keys*

As we saw in Unit 1, all nouns in Spanish are either masculine or feminine and, as in English, there are singular and plural forms. Likewise, the definite article (*the*) has different forms depending on the gender (masculine or feminine) and number (singular or plural) of the noun it qualifies:

el hotel (masc. sing.)   *the hotel*
la habitación (fem. sing.)   *the room*
los hoteles (masc. pl.)   *the hotels*
las habitaciones (fem. pl.)   *the rooms*

But before a feminine noun beginning with a stressed **a-** or **ha-** we must use **el** and not **la**.

el agua   *water*
el arte   *art*
el hambre   *hunger*

The noun, however, is still feminine. Notice:

el agua fría   *cold water*

las aguas   *waters*
las artes plásticas   *plastic arts*

Nota: More on the use of the definite article on pages 213–214 of **Apuntes gramaticales**.

4 Interrogative words *quién, cuál, qué*

To ask questions in order to identify people, places and things we may need words such as ¿**quién**? (*who?*), ¿**cuál**? (¿*which?*, *what?*) and ¿**qué**? (*what?*).

Quién – quiénes

Quién translates into English as *who*.

> ¿**Quién** es aquel muchacho?   *Who's that boy?*
> ¿**Quién** es aquella mucha-   *Who's that girl?*
> cha?

If we are referring to more than one person we must use the plural form **quiénes** followed by the plural form of the verb.

> ¿**Quiénes** son esas personas?   *Who are those people?*
> ¿**Quiénes** son esos niños?   *Who are those children?*

Cuál – cuáles

The most usual translation of **cuál** into English is *which*, as in:

> ¿**Cuál** es la maleta?   *Which is the suitcase?*
> ¿**Cuál** es el equipaje?   *Which is the luggage?*

The Spanish equivalent of *which are . . . ?* is ¿**cuáles son** . . . ?, as in:

> ¿**Cuáles son** los billetes?   *Which are the tickets?*
> ¿**Cuáles son** las cartas?   *Which are the letters?*

Notice also the use of **cuál** – **cuáles** in sentences where English would normally require the use of *what*:

¿**Cuál** es el problema?	*What's the problem?*
¿**Cuál** es la razón?	*What's the reason?*

Remember: The English construction *what* + *to be* + *noun* normally translates into Spanish as ¿**cuál es** . . . ?, ¿**cuáles son** . . . ?

Qué

Qué translates normally as *what*, for example

¿**Qué** es eso?	*What's that?*
¿**Qué** es esto?	*What's this?*

But when it functions as an adjective, it sometimes translates as *which*:

¿**Qué** libro es?	*Which book is it?*
¿**Qué** habitación es?	*Which room is it?*

Notice the use of the accent in all interrogative words: ¿**quién**?, ¿**cuál**?, ¿**qué**?, etc.

5 Possessive adjective *mi*

The Spanish equivalent of *my*, as in *my friend*, varies in number depending on whether the noun which follows is singular or plural, but there is no variation for masculine or feminine.

Ésta es **mi** amiga Isabel	*This is my friend Isabel*
Éstos son **mis** amigos chilenos	*These are my Chilean friends*

Nota: For the full forms and usage of possessive adjectives and pronouns see Unit 6.

En contexto

1 *Study these conversations in which people are being introduced. The first exchange is informal and the second one formal.*

(*a*) **Cristina** ¿Qué tal Isabel?
   Isabel   Hola Cristina, ¿cómo estás?
   Cristina Bien, gracias. Ésta es Gloria, mi amiga argentina.
   Isabel   Hola.
   Gloria   Hola.

¿qué tal?	*how are you?* (informal)
¿cómo estás?	*how are you?* (informal)
bien, gracias	*fine, thank you*

(*b*) **Señora Gómez** Buenas tardes, señor Ramos. ¿Cómo está Vd.?
   Señor Ramos Muy bien, ¿y Vd.?
   Señora Gómez Bien, gracias. Éste es José, mi marido.
   Señor Ramos Mucho gusto, señor
   Señor Gómez Encantado.

¿cómo está Vd.?	*how are you?* (formal)
muy bien	*very well*

---

2 *Getting to know people*

Rodolfo ¿Quién es aquella chica?
Alvaro ¿Cuál?
Rodolfo Aquella chica de azul.
Alvaro Ésa es Marta. Es guapa, ¿eh?
Rodolfo Sí, muy guapa.

---

de azul	*in blue*
guapo/a	*pretty, good looking*

Explicaciones

Encantado (masculine) and **encantada** (feminine), meaning *pleased to meet you*, vary in gender depending on whether the speaker is a man or a woman. **Mucho gusto**, which has a similar meaning, is invariable. A more informal greeting is **hola**, *hello*.

Expansión

1 Other ways of introducing people

In Spanish, as in English, people may be introduced in more than one way. Think of the alternatives in English, for example

> *This is John*
> *Have you met Sarah?*
> *May I introduce my wife?*
> *I'd like you to meet my son David*

So far, we have learnt the most simple and perhaps the most common way of introducing people in Spanish, e.g. **éste es Antonio**, *this is Antonio*. But there are other ways. Learn them as set phrases at this stage, without thinking of them in terms of their grammatical construction.

Te presento a Juan (informal)	*May I introduce Juan*
Le presento a María (formal)	*May I introduce Maria*
¿Conoces a Ana? (informal)	*Do you know* (or *have you met*) *Ana?*
¿Conoce Vd. a Dolores? (formal)	*Do you know* or *have you met*) *Dolores?*

2 Identifying what you want

The neuter demonstratives **esto** and **eso** may come in particularly handy when you don't know the Spanish equivalent of what you want, at a shop or restaurant for example.

Esto por favor	*This please*
Eso por favor	*That please*
Quiero **esto** por favor	*I want this please*
Quiero **eso** por favor	*I want that please*

3 Describing people, places and things

Objetivos

In this Unit you will learn how to:

Describe people • Describe places • Describe things
• Ask questions leading to the description of people, places
and things • Describe the weather

Contenido gramatical

'Ser' in description • 'Estar' in description • Adjectives
• Interrogative word '¿cómo?' • 'Hacer' in description of
the weather • 'Tener' in description

Nota preliminar

To describe people, places or things in general terms, as in *Gloria is
tall*, *Madrid is a big city*, *it's nice*, etc. Spanish normally uses a
construction with **ser** (*to be*) followed by an adjective: **Gloria es alta,
Madrid es una ciudad grande, Es bonito.**

To ask questions leading to the description of people, places or
things, as in *what is it like?*, we use the construction **¿cómo + ser**
(+ noun)?: **¿cómo es?**

To describe people, places and things at a particular point in time and with regard to a state or condition, we use **estar** (see below) rather than **ser**, followed by a descriptive adjective, for example

Marta está guapa	*Marta looks pretty*
La casa está sucia hoy	*the house is (looks) dirty today*

To describe the weather, Spanish normally uses the verb **hacer** (*to do*, *make*) plus a noun, as in **hace frío**, *it's cold*, **hace calor**, *it's warm*.

Have a look at these examples and their English translation before going on to the **Resumen gramatical**.

Describing people, places and things

Roberto es simpático	*Roberto is nice*
María Inés es baja	*María Inés is short*
Sitges es pequeño	*Sitges is small*
Bilbao es industrial	*Bilbao is industrial*
El coche es cómodo	*The car is comfortable*
Las maletas son finas	*The suitcases are good*

Asking questions leading to the description of people, places and things

¿Cómo es Roberto?	*What's Roberto like?*
¿Cómo es Sitges?	*What's Sitges like?*
¿Cómo son las maletas?	*What are the suitcases like?*

Describing people, places and things at a particular point in time

Andrés está aburrido	*Andrés is bored*
La habitación está limpia	*The room is clean*
Mis gafas están sucias	*My glasses are dirty*

Describing the weather

Hace (mucho) frío	*It's (very) cold*
Hace (demasiado) calor	*It's (too) hot*
Hace (un poco de) viento	*It's (a little) windy*

Resumen gramatical

1 *Ser* and *estar* (to be)

There are two ways of saying *to be* in Spanish – **ser** and **estar** – and the uses of each are clearly differentiated by the native speaker, as you will see from the explanations and examples below.

Nota: see also pages 227–229 of **Apuntes gramaticales**.

2 *Ser* used in description

Ser is the verb most frequently used in description. In this context, it is generally used with adjectives which refer to:

(*a*) Characteristics which are considered as permanent, e.g. physical and mental characteristics.

Víctor **es** delgado	*Victor is thin*
Mercedes **es** inteligente	*Mercedes is intelligent*

(*b*) Characteristics which, although subjective, may be considered as true by the speaker.

El español **es** fácil	*Spanish is easy*
El árabe **es** difícil	*Arabic is difficult*

(*c*) Characteristics which are considered as universal.

La Tierra **es** redonda	*The earth is round*
El oro **es** un metal	*Gold is a metal*

(*d*) Certain states or conditions such as **inocente** (*innocent*), **culpable** (*guilty*), **pobre** (*poor*), **feliz** (*happy*), **desgraciado** (*unhappy*).

Ella **es** inocente	*She's innocent*
Ellos **son** felices	*They're happy*
Son países pobres	*They're poor countries*

Nota: For other uses of **ser** see Units 5, 6, 11 and pages 227–228 of **Apuntes gramaticales**.

3   *Estar* used in description

Estar is not normally used in description, except with adjectives which refer to a state or condition, for example:

Estás elegante	*You look elegant*
Cecilia **está** triste	*Cecilia is (looks) sad*
Ricardo **está** contento	*Ricardo is happy*

Some adjectives may be used with either **ser** or **estar**. **Ser** refers to the nature of what is being described while **estar** denotes a state or condition at a particular point in time. Consider these sentences:

Jorge **es** elegante	*Jorge is elegant* (always)
Jorge **está** elegante	*Jorge is (looks) elegant* (now)
Mónica **es** gorda	*Mónica is fat* (general characteristic)
Mónica **está** gorda	*Mónica is fat* (now)

Nota: It is not correct to say – as stated in some textbooks – that **ser** always refers to permanent characteristics while **estar** refers to states which are transitory. The following examples defeat that rule:

Mi madre **está** muerta	*My mother is dead*
Cádiz está **en** Andalucía	*Cadiz is in Andalusia*

Present tense of *estar*

Here is **estar** fully conjugated in the present tense:

Singular		Plural	
estoy	*I am*	estamos	*we are*
estás	*you are*	estáis	*you are*
	(familiar)		(familiar)
está	*you are*	están	*you are*
	(polite)		(polite)
	he/she/it is		*they are*

For other uses of **estar** see Units 5 and 8 and pages 228–229 of **Apuntes gramaticales.**

4 Adjectives

To be able to describe things you need adjectives. In Unit 1 we referred specifically to adjectives indicating nationality (pages 6–7). In this Unit we will study the use of adjectives in more general terms, with special emphasis on their descriptive value.

Types of adjectives

According to the kind of agreement they show with the noun which they modify, adjectives may be classified into three different types:

(*a*)   *Adjectives which agree in number and gender with the noun*

Most Spanish adjectives fall in this category and within this group we have most of those ending in -o (e.g. bajo, *short*, pequeño, *small*), -or (e.g. trabajador, *hardworking,* adulador, *flattering*), -án (e.g. holgazán, *lazy*, haragán, *lazy*) as well as some much less frequent adjectives ending in -ín (e.g. malandrín, *perverse*), -ón (e.g. glotón, *gluttonous*), etc.

How to form the feminine

To form the feminine change the final vowel into -a or add -a to the consonant, for example bajo→baja (*short*), trabajador→trabajadora (*hardworking*), holgazán→holgazana (*lazy*).

How to form the plural

To form the plural add -s to the singular form, unless the word ends in a consonant, in which case you add -es, for example pequeño→pequeños (*small*), holgazán→holgazanes (*lazy*).

(*b*) *Adjectives which agree only in number*

Within this group of adjectives, which show no difference between masculine and feminine, are included all those that end in a consonant (note the exceptions above), for instance **azul**, *blue*; **gris**, *grey*; **marrón**, *brown*; **feliz**, *happy*. Other adjectives which fall in this category are those ending in -a (e.g. hipócrita, *hypocritical*), -e (e.g. grande, *big*), -í (e.g. baladí, *trivial*).

How to form the plural

To form the plural, add -s to the final vowel, for example hipócrita→hipócritas (*hypocritical*), unless the word ends in a consonant or in -í, in which case you add -es: gris→grises (grey), baladí→baladíes (*trivial*). To form the plural of adjectives which end in -z change the -z to -c and add -es, for example feliz→felices (*happy*).

Nota: Adjectives which end in -ú, a very infrequent ending in Spanish, also fall within this category, e.g. hindú→hindúes (*Indian*).

(*c*) *Adjectives which are invariable*

A few adjectives do not change for number or gender. Among these we find those which are loan words from other languages, for instance:

un coche **beige**   *a beige car*

una bicicleta **beige**	*a beige bicycle*
unos coches **beige**	*some beige cars*
unas bicicletas **beige**	*some beige bicycles*

Some adjectives describing colour, particularly those which may also function as nouns, e.g. **naranja** (*orange*), **violeta** (*violet*), **rosa** (*pink, rose*), are not normally marked for number and gender. See for example:

| una blusa **naranja** | *an orange blouse* |
| unas blusas **naranja** | *some orange blouses* |

Agreement of adjectives

(*a*) As a general rule, in the presence of one or more than one masculine nouns, use the masculine form of the adjective, e.g. **libros y periódicos españoles**, *Spanish books and newspapers.*

(*b*) In the presence of one or more feminine nouns, use the feminine form of the adjective, e.g. **escuelas y universidades americanas**, *American schools and universities.*

(*c*) If there are nouns of different gender you will need to use the masculine form of the adjective, e.g. **hombres y mujeres chilenos**, *Chilean men and women.*

Short forms

A few adjectives have short forms: **grande** (*large, big*) shortens to **gran** before a masculine or feminine singular noun:

un coche **grande**	*a big car*
un **gran** coche	*a big car*
una ciudad **grande**	*a big city*
una **gran** ciudad	*a big city*

Nota: When **grande** precedes the noun it often translates into English as *great*:

| un **gran** hombre | *a great man* |
| una **gran** mentira | *a great lie* |

Bueno (*good*) and **malo** (*bad*) drop the ending **-o** when they come before a masculine noun:

un libro **bueno**	*a good book*
un **buen** libro	*a good book*
un día **malo**	*a bad day*
un **mal** día	*a bad day*

Intensive forms

To intensify the meaning of a descriptive adjective we can add to it the suffix **-ísimo** (masculine) or **-ísima** (feminine). Adjectives which end in a vowel must drop the vowel before adding **-ísimo/a**. See what happens to **difícil** (*difficult*), **caro** (*expensive*) and **sabroso** (*tasty*) below:

Es dificilísimo	*It's very difficult*
Es carísimo	*It's very expensive*
La comida está sabrosísima	*The food is very tasty*

Notice the following spelling changes when adding **-ísimo/a**. Adjectives which end in **-co**, e.g. **rico** (*rich*) change the **c** to **qu** before adding this suffix.

Él es riquísimo	*He's very rich*

Adjectives which end in **-ble**, e.g. **amable** (*kind*) change **-ble** into **-bil-** before adding **ísimo**.

Ella es amabilísima	*She's very kind*

Other spelling changes affect adjectives which are much less frequently used.

Nota: As there are a number of adjectives which cannot take **-ísimo/a**, it is best not to use this suffix if you're not sure. Instead, you can use an intensifier such as **muy** (*very*), **demasiado** (*too*), or **bastante** (*quite*).

Es **muy** barato	*It's very cheap*
Está **demasiado** caliente	*It's too hot*
Él es **bastante** raro	*He's quite strange*

Position of adjectives

Adjectives often follow the noun they describe:

Es un problema **difícil**	*It's a difficult problem*
Es una chica **alta**	*She's a tall girl*

Descriptive adjectives are sometimes placed before the noun to show emphasis, affection or some other desired effect:

Es una **buena** idea	*It's a good idea*
Es una **pequeña** casa	*It's a small house*

Nota: For comparison of adjectives see pages 217–218 of **Apuntes gramaticales**.

5 Interrogative word ¿*cómo*?

Cómo normally translates into English as *how*, as in questions enquiring about the state or condition of someone or something:

¿**Cómo** está Fernando?	*How's Fernando?*
¿**Cómo** están ellos?	*How are they?*

But in questions leading to the description of people, places or things in terms of their characteristics, **cómo** translates into English as *what*:

¿**Cómo** es Fernando?	*What is Fernando like?*
¿**Cómo** son ellos?	*What are they like?*

Remember: to enquire about a state or condition we use **estar**, while to ask questions regarding characteristics we must use **ser**.

6 *Hacer* in description of the weather

To describe the weather Spanish normally uses the verb **hacer** (literally, *to do*, *make*) in the 3rd person singular plus a noun.

Hace (mucho) frío	*It's very cold*
Hace (demasiado) calor	*It's too hot*
Hace (un poco de) viento	*It's (a little) windy*

En contexto

1 *Describing someone.*

A ¿Quién es ese señor?
B Es el nuevo profesor de español.
A ¿Cómo es?
B Es simpático, pero es muy estricto.
A ¿Es buen profesor?
B Sí, es un profesor excelente.

nuevo	*new*
el profesor de español	*Spanish teacher*
estricto	*strict*

2 *Read this extract from a letter describing a place.*

Querido Jorge,

Esta es mi primera visita a Cadaqués. Es un lugar precioso y el hotel es estupendo, aunque es un poco caro. Hace muchísimo calor ...

mi primera visita	*my first visit*
un lugar precioso	*a very nice place*
aunque	*although*

Explicaciones

Ésta es mi primera visita a Cadaqués. Notice the position of the ordinal number **primera**. Ordinal numbers normally precede the noun they qualify.

Expansión

1 *Tener* in description

In Spanish, as in English, the ways in which we describe things can be quite varied. So far in this Unit we have studied the uses of **ser** and **estar** within the context of description. But we can also use other verbs in the same context. Consider, for instance, the use of **tener** (*to have*) in these examples:

Adela **tiene** ojos verdes	*Adela has green eyes*
Alberto **tiene** pelo negro	*Alberto has black hair*
El hotel Plaza **tiene** dos bares	*The hotel Plaza has two bars*
Las habitaciones **tienen** teléfono	*The rooms have a telephone*

Tiene (*you have, he/she/it has*) and **tienen** (*you/they have*) are frequently used to refer to the characteristics of people, places and things. For the full forms and other uses of **tener** see Units 4 and 6.

2 Describing things in terms of the material they are made of

To describe things in relation to the material they are made of we use the verb **ser**: **es de** . . . in the singular and **son de** . . . in the plural.

Es de madera	*It's made of wood*
Es de metal	*It's made of metal*
Son de oro	*They're made of gold*
Son de lana	*They're made of wool*

3 Other ways of describing the weather

Although the weather is normally described with **hacer**, e.g. **hace frío** (*it's cold*), the climate in general may be described with the verb **ser** followed by an adjective.

El clima **es** (muy) frío	*The climate is (very) cold*
El clima **es** (muy) caluroso	*The climate is (very) hot*
El clima **es** templado	*The climate is mild*

Tener may also be used in this context:

Galicia **tiene** un clima húmedo	*Galicia has a wet climate*
Valencia **tiene** un clima mediterráneo	*Valencia has a Mediterranean climate*

4 Expressing existence and availability

Objetivos

In this Unit you will learn how to:

Express existence • Enquire about existence • Express availability • Enquire about availability • Ask and answer questions regarding quantity

Contenido gramatical

'Hay' • 'Tener' in the present tense • Indefinite articles • Interrogative word '¿cuánto?' • 'alguien' and 'nadie' • 'alguno' and 'ninguno' • 'algo' and 'nada' • Other verbs expressing existence and availability

Nota preliminar

To ask and answer questions regarding existence you will need the Spanish equivalent of *is there . . . ?*, *are there . . . ? there is . . .*, *there are . . .* Spanish uses a single word to express all this: this word is **hay**.

To ask and answer questions regarding availability, as in *Have you got a room?*, *We have no rooms*, Spanish normally uses the verb **tener** (*to have*).

You will also need the Spanish equivalent of words such as *some, any, none, somebody, nobody, something, nothing*.

To ask questions relating to quantity, as in *How much information is there?* or *How many newspapers are there?*, we need to use the word ¿**cuánto/s**? (*how much/how many?*). To reply to a question like that you will need a phrase such as **un poco** (*a little*), **mucho** (*a lot*), **suficiente** (*enough*), or a number, for example **(hay) dos/tres/cuatro** ((*there are*) *two/three/four*).

Have a look at these examples and their English translation before going on to the **Resumen gramatical**.

Expressing existence

Hay un restaurante	*There's a restaurant*
Hay dos bares	*There are two bars*
No **hay** ninguna habitación	*There isn't a room*
No **hay** habitaciones	*There are no rooms*

Enquiring about existence

¿**Hay** piscina?	*Is there a swimming pool?*
¿**Hay** teléfonos?	*Are there any telephones?*
¿**Hay** alguna farmacia por aquí?	*Is there a chemist's around here?*

Expressing availability

Tengo dos habitaciones libres	*I have two rooms available*
El hotel no **tiene** sauna	*The hotel has no sauna*
No **tenemos** ninguna mesa	*We haven't got a table*

Enquiring about availability

¿**Tiene** Vd. una habitación doble?	*Have you got a double room?*

¿**Tiene** cuarto de baño la habitación?	*Has the room got a bathroom?*
¿**Tienen** Vds. aparcamiento?	*Have you got a car-park?*

Asking and answering questions regarding quantity

¿Cuántos comedores **hay**?	*How many dining rooms are there?*
Hay dos comedores	*There are two dining rooms*
¿Cuánto dinero **hay**?	*How much money is there?*
Hay mucho dinero	*There's a lot of money*
¿Cuántas habitaciones **tiene** el hostal?	*How many rooms has the hostel?*
Tiene quince habitaciones	*It has fifteen rooms*

Resumen gramatical

1 *Hay* (there is/are, is/are there?)

To say *there is* ..., *there are* ..., *is there* ...?, *are there* ...?, Spanish uses the single word **hay**. Hay may be used in positive, negative and interrogative sentences, as you can see from the examples above. In negative sentences **no** precedes the word **hay**. In interrogative sentences simply use the same word as in a statement, but with a rising intonation. Bear in mind that **hay** is invariable and therefore it may be followed by singular or plural nouns. Here are some more examples of its use:

¿**Hay** un supermercado por aquí?	*Is there a supermarket around here?*
Hay uno en la esquina	*There's one at the corner*
Aquí no **hay** supermercados	*There are no supermarkets here*
¿**Hay** teléfonos aquí?	*Are there any telephones here?*

Arriba **hay** dos	*There are two upstairs*
No **hay** ninguno	*There aren't any*

2 *Tener* (to have)

One of several functions of **tener** (*to have*) is the expression of availability. **Tener** is an irregular verb. Its present tense forms are:

Singular		Plural	
tengo	*I have*	tenemos	*we have*
tienes	*you have*	tenéis	*you have*
	(familiar)		(familiar)
tiene	*you have* (polite)	tienen	*you have* (polite)
	he/she/it has		*they have*

Examples:

¿**Tiene** Vd. sellos?	*Have you got any stamps?*
Aquí no **tenemos** sellos	*We have no stamps here*
¿**Tiene** Vd. cambio?	*Have you got any change?*
Lo siento, no **tengo**	*I'm sorry, I haven't*
¿**Tienen** Vds. una habitación individual?	*Have you got a single room?*
Sí, **tenemos**	*Yes, we have*

3 Indefinite articles (a/an)

The word for *a* is **un** for masculine nouns and **una** for feminine nouns.

Masculine:

¿Hay **un** supermercado por aquí?	*Is there a supermarket around here?*
Hay **un** restaurante	*There is a restaurant*

Feminine:

¿Tienen Vds. **una** habitación?   *Have you got a room?*

¿Tiene Vd. **una** mesa?   *Have you got a table?*

The plural forms **unos**, **unas** are translated into English as *some*:

unos restaurantes	*some restaurants*
unas habitaciones	*some rooms*

Spanish does not use the equivalent of English *a* when you indicate your own or someone else's occupation. Compare these phrases:

¿Hay un camarero?	*Is there a waiter?*
Paco es camarero	*Paco is a waiter*
Yo soy recepcionista	*I'm a receptionist*

Nota: see also **Explicaciones** in Unit 1 and pages 214–215 of **Apuntes gramaticales**.

4 Interrogative word *¿cuánto?* (how much/how many?)

As an adjective

In sentences such as ¿**cuánto dinero hay**? (*how much money is there?*) ¿**cuántas habitaciones tiene el hostal**? (*how many rooms has the hostel?*), **cuánto** functions as an adjective and therefore it must agree in number and gender with the noun it modifies. Here are some other examples of its use:

¿**Cuánto** tiempo tenemos?	*How much time have we got?*
¿**Cuánta** fruta hay?	*How much fruit is there?*
¿**Cuántos** invitados hay?	*How many guests are there?*
¿**Cuántas** personas hay?	*How many people are there?*

As a pronoun

Cuánto may also function as a pronoun, in sentences in which the noun is understood. As a pronoun, **cuánto** must also agree in number and gender with the noun it refers to. Here are some examples:

(¿**Cuántos** mercados hay?)	(*How many markets are there?*)
¿**Cuántos** hay?	*How many are there?*
(¿**Cuánta** gente hay?)	(*How many people are there?*)
¿**Cuánta** hay?	*How many are there?*

Here are some words and phrases which may be used to reply to questions with ¿**cuánto/s**?:

Hay mucho/a	*There is a lot*
Hay un poco	*There is a little*
Hay suficiente	*There is enough*
Hay bastante	*There is enough*
Hay muchos/as	*There are many*
Hay pocos/as	*There are a few*
Hay suficientes	*There are enough*
Hay bastantes	*There are enough*

5   *Alguien* (somebody/someone, anybody/anyone)

Alguien is an invariable pronoun which is used in positive and interrogative sentences.

¿Hay **alguien** allí?	*Is there anyone there?*
Hay **alguien** en la puerta	*There's someone at the door*
En el coche hay **alguien**	*There's someone in the car*

6   *Nadie* (nobody/no one)

Nadie is a negative word which may follow the verb, as in:

Allí no hay **nadie**	*There's nobody there*
En la puerta no hay **nadie**	*There's nobody at the door*

Notice that in this construction Spanish must use a double negative.

Nadie may also precede the verb, acting as the subject of a sentence, for example:

Nadie tiene fuego	*No one has a light*
Nadie tiene tiempo	*No one has time*

Notice that in this construction the negative **no** must be omitted.

7 *Alguno* (some/any)

Alguno varies in gender and number according to the noun it modifies (acting as an adjective) or the noun it refers to (acting as a pronoun). Its forms are **algún, alguno, algunos, alguna, algunas**.

Algún

This word is used before a singular masculine noun:

¿Hay **algún** banco por aquí?	*Is there a bank around here?*
¿Hay **algún** museo en la ciudad?	*Is there any museum in the city?*

Alguno/s, alguna/s

Here are some examples of how these words are used:

¿Tiene Vd. **alguno?**	*Have you got any?*
Tenemos **algunos** billetes solamente	*We only have a few tickets*
Ya hay **algunas** personas en la reunión	*There are already some people at the meeting*

Nota: In singular sentences **algún, alguno, alguna** may be replaced by **uno/a**.

¿Hay **algún** café por aquí?	*Is there a café around here?*
¿Hay **un** café por aquí?	*Is there a café around here?*

8   *Ninguno* (no/any/none/nobody)

Ninguno is a negative word which normally occurs in the singular as **ningún** (before masculine nouns), **ninguno** or **ninguna**. This negative word may follow the verb, as in

No hay **ningún** bar	*There isn't a bar*
No hay **ninguno**	*There isn't one*
No tenemos **ninguna** reserva	*We have no reservation*
No tenemos **ninguna**	*We don't have one*

Notice that in this construction Spanish must use a double negative.

Ninguno may sometimes precede the verb, as in:

Ningún banco tiene cajero automático	*No bank has a cash point*
Ninguno tiene cajero automático	*None of them has a cash point*

9   *Algo* (some/any/something/anything)

Algo is an invariable pronoun which normally follows the verb.

¿Hay **algo** de dinero?	*Is there any money?*
Hay **algo**	*There is some*
¿Hay **algo** de comer?	*Is there something to eat?*
Todavía hay **algo**	*There's still something left*

10   *Nada* (nothing/any)

Nada is a negative word which normally follows the verb.

No hay **nada** de carne	*There isn't any meat*
No hay **nada**	*There is nothing*

Notice the double negative in this construction.

En contexto

1   *Study this conversation between a tourist and a hotel receptionist.*

Recepcionista	Buenos días.
Turista	Buenos días. ¿Tiene alguna habitación?
Recepcionista	¿Para cuántas personas?
Turista	Para dos.
Recepcionista	Tenemos una interior solamente. Exterior no tenemos ninguna.
Turista	Está bien.

para	*for*
una (habitación) interior	*a room at the back*
una (habitación) exterior	*a room facing the street*
está bien	*it's all right*

2   *Read this text describing the facilities available at a hotel.*

El Hotel Don Carlos es un hotel de cuatro estrellas. El hotel tiene cien habitaciones dobles, treinta individuales y cuatro suites. Todas las habitaciones tienen baño privado, teléfono y televisor.

En el Hotel Don Carlos hay tres restaurantes y dos bares. También hay una piscina muy grande y una sauna. El hotel tiene aparcamiento propio para los clientes. Además, hay una sala de convenciones muy cómoda y moderna para trescientas personas.

un hotel de cuatro estrellas	*a four-star hotel*
todos/as	*all*
el baño privado	*private bathroom*
el televisor	*TV set*
también	*also*
propio	*own*
los clientes	*clients, customers*
además	*besides*
una sala de convenciones	*a conference room*

Explicaciones

(a) Tenemos una interior   *We have one at the back only*
     solamente

Una here stands for **una habitación**.

(b) Exterior no tenemos   *We haven't got any facing the*
     ninguna   *street*

Notice the alternative word order: **no tenemos ninguna exterior**. In the
former sentence the emphasis is on exterior.

(c) Notice the use of **para** in the following phrases:

    ¿**para** cuántas personas?   *for how many people?*
    para dos personas   *for two people*
    para los clientes   *for the clients*
    para 300 personas   *for 300 people*

Expansión

1   Other verbs expressing existence and availability

Existence and availability may also be expressed using other less
frequent verbs:

Existir (literally, *to exist*)

    En Madrid **existen**   *In Madrid there are excellent*
    excelentes museos   *museums*
    Existen muy buenos hoteles   *There are many good hotels*

Nota: **Existir** is a regular 3rd conjugation verb (see page 72).

Contar con (*to have*)

La ciudad **cuenta con** un buen sistema de transporte	*The city has a good transport system*
Las universidades **cuentan con** centros deportivos	*The universities have sport centres*

Nota: **Contar** is a stem-changing verb in which **o** changes into **ue** (see page 75).

Disponer de (*to have*)

El ayuntamiento **dispone de** poco dinero	*The town hall has little money*
La ciudad no **dispone de** buenas bibliotecas	*The city doesn't have good libraries*

Nota: **Disponer** is conjugated like **poner** (see page 73).

5 Expressing location

Objetivos

In this Unit you will learn how to:

Express location • Express distance • Ask questions regarding location and distance • Ask and answer questions regarding the location of events • Give simple directions

Contenido gramatical

'Estar' in the expression of location and distance • Interrogative word '¿dónde?' • Words and phrases used in the expression of location and distance • 'Ser' to refer to the location of events • Other verbs denoting location

Nota preliminar

To give information regarding location, as in *It's in the square*, we can use the verb **estar** (*to be*) followed by a preposition: **Está en la plaza**.

Distance, as in *It's two streets away*, is normally expressed with **estar** followed by the preposition **a**: **Está a dos calles de aquí**.

To ask questions regarding location, for example *Where's the market?*, Spanish normally uses the construction ¿**dónde** + **estar** + noun?: **¿Dónde está el mercado?**

To enquire about distance we may use phrases such as these:

¿A qué distancia está?	*How far is it?*
¿Está lejos/cerca?	*Is it far/near?*

To be able to give information about location and to give simple directions you will need words and phrases like **en** (*in*), **detrás de** (*behind*), **enfrente de** (*opposite*), etc. These and other similar words will be listed under the grammar notes.

Have a look at these examples and their English translation before going on to the **Resumen gramatical**.

Expressing location

El mercado está en la esquina	*The market is at the corner*
Correos está allí	*The post office is there*
Los teléfonos están abajo	*The telephones are downstairs*

Expressing distance

Madrid está a 500 km de aquí	*Madrid is 500 km from here*
La iglesia está a dos calles de aquí	*The church is two streets from here*
El aeropuerto está lejos	*The airport is a long way away*

Asking questions regarding location and distance

¿Dónde está la oficina de turismo?	*Where's the tourist office?*
¿Dónde están los servicios?	*Where are the toilets?*
¿A qué distancia está Burgos?	*How far is Burgos?*
¿Está cerca la plaza?	*Is the square nearby?*

Asking and answering questions regarding the location of events

¿Dónde es la reunión?	*Where's the meeting?*
Es en mi despacho	*It's in my office*
¿Dónde es la fiesta?	*Where's the party?*
Es aquí	*It's here*

Giving simple directions

¿Dónde está la estación, por favor?	*Where's the station, please?*
Está al final de esta calle, a la derecha	*It's at the end of this street, on the right*
¿Dónde está el museo?	*Where's the museum?*
Está a cinco minutos de aquí, enfrente de la catedral	*It's five minutes from here, opposite the cathedral*

Resumen gramatical

1 *Estar* in the expression of location and distance

Estar (*to be*) is the verb most frequently used in Spanish when expressing location and distance. It is normally used in the third person singular or plural, followed immediately by a preposition, e.g. **en** (*in, on, at*), **entre** (*between*) or an adverb of place, e.g. **aquí** (*here*), **allí** (*there*), **enfrente** (*opposite*). (For the full forms of **estar** see Unit 3). Examples:

Mi familia **está en** Inglaterra	*My family is in England*
Los viajeros **están en** el avión	*The travellers are in the aeroplane*
La panadería **está** allí **enfrente**	*The baker's is over there*

La carnicería **está al lado de**
la farmacia

The butcher's is next to the
chemist's

Sometimes **estar** may be used with other persons of the verb, as in

Estoy en la cocina
Estamos en París

I'm in the kitchen
We're in Paris

Nota: See also pages 228–229 of **Apuntes gramaticales.**

2 Interrogative word *¿dónde?*

Dónde (*where*), as an interrogative word, is used to enquire about location. It normally precedes the third person singular or plural of **estar**, but it may also be used with other persons of the verb. Here are some examples:

¿**Dónde** está Bilbao?
Está en el norte
¿**Dónde** están las Baleares?
Están en el Mediterráneo

Where's Bilbao?
It's in the north
Where are the Balearics?
They are in the
Mediterranean

¿**Dónde** están tus amigos?
Están en México
¿**Dónde** estás?
Estoy en el jardín

Where are your friends?
They are in Mexico
Where are you?
I'm in the garden

3 Words and phrases used in the expression of location and distance

To be able to give information about location and distance you will need prepositions. Prepositions are words like **a**, e.g. está **a** cinco minutos (*it's five minutes away*), **en**, e.g. está **en** el parque (*it's in the park*), **entre**, e.g. está **entre** el banco y correos (*it's between the bank and the post office*). Certain prepositions combine with adverbs of place, words like **detrás** (*behind*), **enfrente** (*opposite*), to form set phrases used in the expression of location, for example, está **detrás** del mercado (*it's behind the market*), está **enfrente** de la iglesia (*it's opposite the church*). We'll call these compound prepositions. Here is a list of the most common simple and compound prepositions used in the context of location and distance.

a (*on, to*)

Está **a** la izquierda/derecha	*It's on the left/right*
Está **a** la izquierda de la calle Mayor	*It's to the left of the calle Mayor*
Está **a** dos manzanas* de aquí	*It's two blocks from here*
Está **a** diez minutos del centro	*It's ten minutes from the centre*
Está **a** 20 km de aquí	*It's 20 km from here*

en (*in, on, at*)

Está **en** la calle Alfonso X	*It's in Alfonso X Street*
Está **en** la mesa	*It's on the table*
Él está **en** la escuela	*He's at school*

entre (*between*)

La universidad está **entre** la iglesia y el banco	*The university is between the church and the bank*

sobre (*on, over, on top of, above*)

Está **sobre** el escritorio	*It's on the desk*
Está **sobre** la ciudad	*It's over the city*
Está **sobre** él	*It's on top of him*
Está **sobre** tu cabeza	*It's above your head*

Nota: notice that **en** and **sobre** are interchangeable in **está sobre/en el escritorio** (*it's on the desk*).

* The Spanish word for *block* in Latin America is **cuadra**.

al final de (*at the end of*)

> La tienda está **al final de** la calle
>
> *The shop is at the end of the street*

al lado de (*next to*)

> Mi casa está **al lado de** la estación
>
> *My house is next to the station*

cerca de (*near*)

> El cine está **cerca del** mercado
>
> *The cinema is near the market*

debajo de (*under, underneath*)

> Los zapatos están **debajo de** la cama
>
> *The shoes are under the bed*

dentro de (*within, inside*)

> El perro está **dentro de** la casa
>
> *The dog is inside the house*

detrás de (*behind*)

> La gasolinera está **detrás de** la estación
>
> *The service station is behind the station*

enfrente de (*opposite*)

> La zapatería está **enfrente de** la papelería
>
> *The shoe shop is opposite the stationer's*

fuera de (*outside*)

> El portero está **fuera del** edificio
>
> *The porter is outside the building*

lejos de (*far*)

Sevilla está **lejos de** Bilbao   *Seville is far from Bilbao*

The following adverbs are frequently used in sentences which express location:

aquí (*here*)

El billete está **aquí**   *The ticket is here*

allí (*there*)

Correos está **allí**   *The post office is there*

ahí (*there*)

Carlos está **ahí**   *Carlos is there*

Nota: **Ahí** indicates closer proximity than **allí**.

The following two forms, although known and used in Spain, are much more frequent in Latin America:

acá (*here*)

Cristina está **acá**   *Cristina is here*

allá (*there*)

La oficina de turismo está **allá**   *The tourist office is there*

4   *Ser* to refer to the location of events

To ask and answer questions regarding the location of events, as in *Where's the party?* and *The party is in my flat*, we use **ser** rather than **estar**. Here are some examples:

¿Dónde **es** la fiesta?	*Where's the party?*
La fiesta **es** en mi piso	*The party is in my flat*
¿Dónde **es** la clase?	*Where's the class?*
La clase **es** aquí	*The class is here*

Remember: When *to be* means *to be held* or *to happen* it must be translated into Spanish as **ser**. (See also page 227 of **Apuntes gramaticales.**)

En contexto

1 *Looking for a bank.*

Turista Perdone, ¿Hay algún banco por aquí?
Guardia Sí, hay uno en la calle Mayor.
Turista ¿Dónde está la calle Mayor?
Guardia Es la segunda calle a la izquierda. El banco está al lado del cine.
Turista Muchas gracias.
Guardia De nada.

la segunda calle	*the second street*
el guardia	*policeman*

2 *On the way to the airport.*

Conductor Perdone, ¿cuál es la carretera para el aeropuerto?
Transeúnte Es la próxima a la derecha.
Conductor ¿A qué distancia está el aeropuerto más o menos?
Transeúnte Está a unos veinte kilómetros.
Conductor Muchas gracias.
Transeúnte No hay de qué.

el conductor	*driver*
el transeúnte	*passer-by*
la carretera	*highway*
la próxima	*next one*
más o menos	*more or less*
no hay de qué	*don't mention it*
unos	*about*

Explicaciones

When you stop someone in the street to ask for directions you can use any of the following words: **perdone** (*excuse me*), **oiga** (*excuse me*) or **por favor** (*please*). Although **oiga** translates literally into English as *listen!*, its use is acceptable in Spain. In some parts of Latin America, however, it may sound abrupt and impolite.

Expansión

1 Other verbs denoting location

Encontrarse, hallarse (*to be, to be situated*)

Estar is not the only verb denoting location. There are other less common verbs which are found in more formal contexts; among these are **encontrarse** and **hallarse** (*to be, to be situated*). Both are reflexive verbs (see Unit 9) and **encontrarse** is also a stem-changing verb (see Unit 8). Here are some examples of how these verbs are used:

¿Dónde se **encuentra** Perú?   *Where's Peru?*
Perú se **encuentra** en   *Peru is in South America*
   América del Sur

¿Dónde se **encuentran** las islas Baleares?	*Where are the Balearic Islands?*
Las islas Baleares se **encuentran** en el Mediterráneo	*The Balearic Islands are in the Mediterranean*
¿Dónde se **halla** Tenerife?	*Where's Tenerife?*
Tenerife se **halla** en las islas Canarias	*Tenerife is in the Canary Islands*
¿Dónde se **hallan** las islas Galápagos?	*Where are the Galápagos Islands?*
Las islas Galápagos se **hallan** en el Pacífico	*The Galápagos Islands are in the Pacific*

Estar situado (*to be situated*)

Location may also be expressed with the construction ¿**dónde** + **estar** + **situado**?; **situado** must agree in gender and number with the noun it refers to.

¿Dónde **está situado** Madrid?	*Where's Madrid situated?*
Madrid **está situado** en el centro de España	*Madrid is situated in the centre of Spain*
¿Dónde **están situados** los Andes?	*Where are the Andes situated?*
Los Andes **están situados** en América del Sur	*The Andes are situated in South America*

6 Expressing possession

Objetivos

In this Unit you will learn how to:
Express possession • Ask questions regarding possession

Contenido gramatical

Possessive adjectives • Possessive pronouns • Preposition 'de' to indicate possession • 'Ser' in the expression of possession • 'Tener' in the expression of possession • Definite article to express possession • Saying of mine, yours, his ... • 'Pertenecer'

Nota preliminar

To express possession you will need the Spanish equivalent of words such as *my, your, his* . . . , as in *my house, his car*. These are called possessive adjectives. You will also need the equivalent of words like *mine, yours, his, hers* . . . , as found in sentences like *This book is mine*, or *That magazine is yours*. Such words are known as possessive pronouns. Sentences like *Peter's friend, Sarah's mother* are expressed in Spanish through the preposition **de**, which in this context means *of* or *belonging to*: **el amigo de Peter, la madre de Sarah.**

You will also learn the Spanish equivalent of questions such as *whose is (it)?, who does (it) belong to?* Attention will also be drawn to the use of **ser** in expressing possession.

In Unit 3 we studied the use of **tener** (*to have*) in description and in Unit 4 we saw how the same verb could be used to express availability. In this Unit we find **tener** in sentences which express possession.

Have a look at these examples and their English translation before going on to the **Resumen gramatical**.

Expressing possession

Ésta es **mi** casa	*This is my house*
Éste es **tu** bolso	*This is your bag*
Nuestro coche es azul	*Our car is blue*
Aquel dinero es **mío**	*That money is mine*
Esa revista es **tuya**	*That magazine is yours*
La maleta marrón es **suya**	*The brown suitcase is yours/his/hers*
La casa **de Rodrigo** está lejos	*Rodrigo's house is far away*
La oficina **del señor Rosas** está arriba	*Señor Rosas's office is upstairs*
La hija **de la señora García** se llama Magdalena	*Señora García's daughter is called Magdalena*
Tiene un piso muy bonito	*She/he has a very nice flat*
Tengo un ordenador nuevo	*I have a new computer*
Tienen mucho dinero	*They have a lot of money*

Asking questions regarding possession

¿**De quién** es este equipaje?	*Whose luggage is this?*
¿**De quién** son estas maletas?	*Whose suitcases are these?*
¿**A quién** pertenece esta propiedad?	*Who does this property belong to?*
¿**A quién** pertenecen esos documentos?	*Who do those documents belong to?*
¿**Tiene** Vd. coche?	*Have you got a car?*

> ¿**Tienen** Vds. una casa en
> España?

> *Have you got a house in*
> *Spain?*

Resumen gramatical

1   Possessive adjectives (my, your, his, her . . .)

To express possession we may, as in English, use possessive adjectives. Possessive adjectives precede a noun or noun phrase, **mi camisa** (*my shirt*), **mis zapatos negros** (*my black shoes*) and they agree in number with the noun that they accompany, but only those ending in **-o** in the masculine singular (**nuestro, vuestro**) agree in gender.

Forms of possessive adjectives		
mi	mis	*my*
tu	tus	*your* (familiar)
su	sus	*your* (formal)/*his/her/its*
nuestro/a	nuestros/as	*our*
vuestro/a	vuestros/as	*your* (familiar)
su	sus	*your* (formal)
		their

Examples:

> Ésta es **mi** chaqueta
> Ésos son **mis** guantes
> **Nuestro** hijo está en Nueva
>   York
> ¿Dónde está **vuestra** familia?

> *This is my jacket*
> *Those are my gloves*
> *Our son is in New York*
>
> *Where's your family?*

2   Possessive pronouns (mine, yours, his, hers . . .)

Possession can also be expressed by means of possessive pronouns, which follow the noun or stand by themselves. All possessive pronouns agree in number and gender with the noun possessed.

Forms of possessive pronouns		
mío/a	míos/as	*mine*
tuyo/a	tuyos/as	*yours* (familiar)
suyo/a	suyos/as	*yours* (polite)/*his/hers/its*
nuestro/a	nuestros/as	*ours*
vuestro/a	vuestros/as	*yours* (familiar)
suyo/a	suyos/as	*yours* (polite)/*theirs*

Examples:

Este libro es **mío**	*This book is mine*
El bolígrafo rojo es **tuyo**	*The red ball-point pen is yours*
Las maletas negras son **nuestras**	*The black suitcases are ours*
La idea **suya** es estupenda	*Your idea is great*

Notice also the use of possessive pronouns with definite articles:

Aquí está tu pasaporte. ¿Dónde está el mío?	*Here's your passport. Where's mine?*
¿Dónde será la fiesta, en la casa de Carlos o en la tuya?	*Where will the party be, in Carlos's house or in yours?*
Tus zapatos son muy elegantes. Los tuyos también	*Your shoes are very elegant. So are yours*

3 Preposition *de* to indicate possession

Another frequent way of expressing possession in Spanish is by using phrases such as these:

El vestido **de Patricia** es nuevo	*Patricia's dress is new*
Me gusta la falda **de Susana**	*I like Susana's skirt*

Los pantalones **de Mario**   *Mario's trousers are very*
son muy modernos   *modern*

¿De quién? (whose)

The Spanish equivalent of *whose is . . . ?*, *whose are . . . ?* is **¿de quién es . . . ?**, **¿de quién son . . . ?** Here are some examples:

¿De quién es ese bolso?   *Whose is that handbag?*
Es de Antonia   *It's Antonia's*
¿De quién son esos libros?   *Whose books are those?*
Son míos   *They're mine*
¿De quién es esto?   *Whose is this?*
Es de mi hermano   *It's my brother's*

4   *Ser* in the expression of possession

Notice that the verb *to be* in sentences like *It's mine*, *They're ours*, *Whose is it?* translates into Spanish as **ser** rather than **estar**. Here are some more examples:

¿Es suyo ese dinero?   *Is that money yours?*
No, no **es** mío   *No, it isn't mine*
Es de Pedro   *It's Pedro's*
¿Son tuyas **estas** llaves?   *Are these keys yours?*
Sí, **son** las mías   *Yes, they're mine*

Nota: See also page 227 of **Apuntes gramaticales**.

5   *Tener* in the expression of possession

Tener (*to have*) can also be used to express possession. Look at these examples:

¿Cuánto dinero **tiene** Vd.?   *How much money have you got?*

Tengo diez mil pesetas   *I have ten thousand pesetas*

| ¿**Tienes** una casa o un piso? | *Have you got a house or a flat?* |
| **Tengo** un piso grande | *I have a large flat* |

En contexto

1 *A hotel porter is helping a tourist with her luggage.*

Portero	¿Cuál es su equipaje?
Turista	El mío es aquél.
Portero	¿Este maletín también es suyo?
Turista	No, no es mío, es de mi amiga. El mío es el negro.
Portero	¿Dónde está su coche?
Turista	Está en el aparcamiento.

| **el maletín** | small suitcase |

2 *Talking about the family.*

Marisol	¿Cómo están tus hijos?
Isabel	Muy bien, ¿y los tuyos?
Marisol	Pablo está un poco resfriado, pero Teresa está bien. Ahora está en casa de sus abuelos. Pablo está solo en casa.
Isabel	Los míos están en la piscina con sus amigos.

está un poco resfriado	*he has a slight cold*
sus abuelos	*her grandparents*
solo	*alone*

3 *Alfonso sees a typed note on his desk. It has been left there by his colleague Roberto.*

Alfonso,

Hoy es el cumpleaños de mi mujer y tenemos una
pequeña fiesta en nuestro nuevo apartamento. Tú
eres nuestro invitado de honor. No faltes.
Nuestra dirección es Ismael Valdés Vergara 640 B.

Roberto

hoy	*today*
el cumpleaños	*birthday*
el invitado de honor	*guest of honour*

Explicaciones

1. El mío es aquél   *That one's mine*
   El mío es el negro   *Mine is the black one*
   ¿Y los tuyos?   *And yours?*

Notice here the use of possessive pronouns preceded by the definite
article (**el, los**). In each of these sentences the noun is understood,
therefore it has been omitted: **el (equipaje) mío** (*mine, my luggage*), **el
(maletín) mío** (*mine, my suitcase*), **los (hijos) tuyos** (*yours, your
children*).

2 Con sus amigos   *With their friends*

Notice the ambiguity of this sentence when it is taken out of context.
Only the context makes it clear that **sus amigos** is *their friends* and not

his, her or *your friends.* To avoid this kind of ambiguity we may resort
to phrases like these:

un amigo de Vd./de él/de   *a friend of yours/his/hers/theirs*
  ella/de ellos

Expansión

1 Definite article to express possession

The possessive is often substituted by a definite article when the object
of the sentence is an item of clothing or a part of the body. For
example:

    Ella se lavó **las** manos   *She washed her hands*
    El se quitó **los** zapatos   *He took off his shoes*
    Nos quitamos **las** chaquetas   *We took off our jackets*

2 Saying *of mine, of yours, of his,* etc.

Phrases like *of mine, of yours, of his,* etc., translate into Spanish simply
as **mío, tuyo, suyo** . . . For example:

    Unos amigos **míos**   *Some friends of mine*
    Una tía **tuya**   *An aunt of yours*
    Un primo **nuestro**   *A cousin of ours*

3 *Pertenecer* (to belong)

Although it is less frequent, possession may also be expressed with
pertenecer (*to belong*).

    ¿A quién **pertenece** esta   *Who does this house belong*
      casa?   *to?*

Pertenece a un señor muy rico	*It belongs to a very rich gentleman*
¿A quién **pertenecen** esos edificios?	*Who do those buildings belong to?*
Pertenecen a una firma inglesa	*They belong to an English firm*

Nota: **pertenecer** is conjugated like **conocer**, *to know* (see page 73).

7   Expressing obligation and needs

Objetivos

In this Unit you will learn how to:

Express obligation and needs • Ask questions with regard to obligation and needs

Contenido gramatical

'tener que' • 'necesitar' • 'deber' • 'hay que' • 'hacer falta' • 'ser necesario' • present tense of 1st and 2nd conjugation verbs

Nota preliminar

As in English, the same constructions may be used in Spanish to express both obligation and need. Consider for instance these sentences: *I have to work harder, She needs to study, One has to accept it* and *We must go*. The line which separates obligation from need is not always clear, therefore in the notes and examples below both functions will be covered simultaneously. You will learn how to express obligation and need with regard to yourself and others, as well as ask whether others are obliged, or need, to do something.

Several verbs cover these functions in Spanish (e.g. **tener que**, *to have to* or **necesitar**, *to need*) and each one of them will be dealt with separately. As in English, these verbs are used with an infinitive (e.g.

tengo que ir, *I have to go* or **necesito trabajar,** *I need to work*) but some may also be followed by a noun or a pronoun (e.g. **necesito dinero,** *I need money* or **necesito éste,** *I need this one*).   Have a look at these examples and their English translation before going on to the **Resumen gramatical**.

Expressing obligation and need

With regard to oneself:

Tengo que salir	*I have to go out*
Necesito estudiar más	*I need to study more*
Debo leer ese libro	*I must read that book*

With regard to others:

Pablo **tiene** que volver	*Pablo has to return*
Elena **necesita** descansar	*Elena needs to rest*
Tú **debes** estar aquí a las 6.00	*You must be here at 6.00*

Expressing obligation and need in impersonal terms

Hay que hacer un esfuerzo	*One has to make an effort*
Hace falta tener paciencia	*One needs to have patience*
Es necesario esperar	*It's necessary to wait*

Asking questions with regard to obligation and need

¿**Qué tienes** que hacer?	*What do you have to do?*
¿**Qué necesitáis**?	*What do you need?*
¿**Qué debo** decir?	*What must I say?*

Resumen gramatical

1 *Tener que* (to have to)

Tener que is the verb most frequently used in the expression of obligation and need. As in English, it is used with an infinitive:

¿Qué **tienes que** hacer?	*What do you have to do?*
Tengo que trabajar	*I have to work*
¿Qué **tenéis que** comprar?	*What do you have to buy?*
Tenemos que comprar pan	*We have to buy bread*
¿Dónde **tienen que** ir Vds.?	*Where do you have to go?*
Tenemos que ir al banco	*We have to go to the bank*

Nota: For the full forms of **tener** in the present tense see Unit 4.

2 *Necesitar* (to need) and present tense of 1st conjugation verbs

To say what we need or what we need to do, we may use **necesitar** (*to need*), followed by a noun, e.g. **necesito dinero** (*I need money*), a pronoun, e.g. **necesito ésos** (*I need those*) or an infinitive, e.g. **necesito hablar con él** (*I need to speak to him*). **Necesitar** is a regular verb whose infinitive ends in **-ar**. Verbs which finish in **-ar** are known as 1st conjugation verbs.

Here are the present tense forms of **necesitar**. Bear in mind that the endings will be the same for all regular **-ar** verbs.

Singular		**Plural**	
necesito	*I need*	necesitamos	*we need*
necesitas	*you need* (fam.)	necesitáis	*you need* (fam.)
necesita	*you need* (pol.)	necesitan	*you need* (pol.)
	he/she/it needs		*they need*

Examples:

¿Cuánto tiempo **necesitas?**	*How much time do you need?*
Necesito un mes	*I need a month*
¿Qué **necesita** hacer Vd.?	*What do you need to do?*
Necesito reparar el coche	*I need to repair the car*
¿**Necesitan** Vds. hablar con alguien?	*Do you need to talk to somebody?*
Necesitamos hablar con Vd.	*We need to talk to you*

3 *Deber* (must, to have to) and present tense of 2nd conjugation verbs

Deber is followed directly by an infinitive. It is a regular verb whose infinitive ends in **-er**. Verbs which finish in **-er** are known as 2nd conjugation verbs.

Here are the present tense forms of **deber**. Bear in mind that the endings will be the same for all regular **-er** verbs.

	Singular		**Plural**	
debo	*I must, have to*	debemos	*we must, have to*
debes	*you must, have to (fam.)*	debéis	*you must, have to (fam.)*
debe	*you must, have to (pol.)*	deben	*you must, have to (pol.)*
	he/she/it must, has to		*they must, have to*

Examples:

¿Qué **debo** hacer?	*What must I do?*
Debes decir la verdad	*You must tell the truth*
¿Qué **deben** decir?	*What must they say?*
No **deben** decir nada	*They mustn't say anything*
Debemos esperar	*We must wait*

4 *Hay que* (one has to)

Hay (3rd person singular of the present tense of **haber**: the auxiliary verb *to have*) **que** is an impersonal verb form used to express obligation or need and it must be followed by an infinitive. **Hay que** translates into English as *one has to/you have to, one/you must*.

Examples:

¿Cuánto tiempo **hay que** esperar?	*How long does one have to wait?*
Hay que esperar una hora	*One has to wait one hour*
¿Qué **hay que** hacer?	*What do you have to do?*
No **hay que** hacer nada	*You don't have to do anything*
Hay que perdonarle	*One has to forgive him*

En contexto

1 *Enquiring about a visa for a Spanish speaking country.*

Secretaria	Buenos días. ¿Qué desea?
Viajero	¿Qué tengo que hacer para conseguir un visado para Venezuela?
Secretaria	¿Qué pasaporte tiene Vd.?
Viajero	Peruano.
Secretaria	Tiene que rellenar esta solicitud y traer su pasaporte con tres fotografías.
Viajero	¿Necesito traer una carta de mi empresa?
Secretaria	¿Es un viaje de negocios?
Viajero	Sí, es un viaje de negocios.
Secretaria	Sí, en ese caso debe traer una carta de su empresa.

conseguir	to get
un visado	a visa
peruano	Peruvian
rellenar una solicitud	to fill in a form
la empresa	firm
un viaje de negocios	a business trip
en ese caso	in that case

2   *Elena, a secretary, describes her duties in a letter to a friend.*

... hay que estar en la oficina a las 9.00.
Primero tengo que leer la correspondencia
de mi jefe y responder a las cartas más
urgentes. A veces debo asistir a reuniones
y tomar notas y de vez en cuando debo salir
para ir al banco o para visitar a algún
cliente ...

la correspondencia	mail
el jefe	boss
a veces	sometimes
asistir	to attend
tomar notas	to take notes
de vez en cuando	from time to time

Explicaciones

1   Notice the use of **para** in these phrases:

para conseguir un visado   to (in order to) get a visa

para ir al banco
to (in order to) go to the bank

para visitar a algún cliente
to (in order to) visit some client

2 Visitar **a** algún cliente   *To visit some client*

For an explanation of the use of the preposition **a** in this context see page 109.

Expansión

1 Other ways of expressing obligation and need

Hacer falta (*to be necessary*)

Like **hay que**, **hace falta** is an impersonal form, made up of the third person singular of **hacer** (*to do, make*) plus the word **falta** (literally, *lack*). This phrase may be used on its own or it may be followed by an infinitive.

Hace falta más dinero
We need more money (impersonal)

Hace falta trabajar más
One needs to work more

¿Qué **hace falta**?
What do we need? (impersonal)

No **hace falta**
It's not necessary

Ser necesario (*to be necessary*)

Ser necesario (*to be necessary*) is less frequent in Spanish than the equivalent English expression. Here are some examples:

Es necesario
It's necessary

No **es necesario**
It isn't necessary

Es necesario hablar con ella
It's necessary to speak to her

No **es necesario** venir mañana
It's not necessary to come tomorrow

8 Talking about the present

Objetivos

In this Unit you will learn how to:

Describe states which are true in the present • Refer to states which are present but not in progress • Refer to events taking place in the present • Refer to timeless ideas • Ask questions regarding present states and events

Contenido gramatical

3rd conjugation verbs • Irregular verbs • Stem-changing verbs • Present continuous (estar + gerund) • 'Llevar' + gerund • 'Hacer' in time phrases

Nota preliminar

To denote states such as *It's warm today*, *She's ill* and *They're happy*, we use the present tense. Events which are present but not necessarily in progress, for example *What's that noise?* (the noise may no longer be in progress at the moment of speaking) or *I'm coming right away* (something which has not yet taken place), may also be expressed in Spanish using the present tense. Events which are actually taking place in the present, for instance *I'm writing* or *They're working*, may be expressed in Spanish through the present tense or through the present continuous (**estar** + gerund). Timeless actions as well as those in which the time factor is not quite clear, as in *What do you think?* or *He doesn't agree*, are again expressed by means of the present tense.

Have a look at these examples and their English translation before going on to the **Resumen gramatical.**

Describing states which are true in the present

Hoy hace calor	*It's warm today*
Ella está enferma	*She's ill*
Ellos están contentos	*They're happy*

Referring to events which are present but not in progress

Escucha ese ruido	*Listen to that noise*
Alguien llama a la puerta	*Someone's knocking at the door*
Ahora voy	*I'm coming right away*

Referring to events taking place in the present

Escribo a mis padres	*I'm writing to my parents*
Estoy escribiendo a mis padres	*I'm writing to my parents*
El niño duerme	*The child is asleep*
El niño está durmiendo	*The child is sleeping*

Nota: Escribo a mis padres translates literally into English as *I write to my parents*, and **el niño duerme** as *the child sleeps*. Only the context would make it clear that these two sentences refer to events which are actually taking place in the present. Such ambiguity does not occur in sentences with **estar** + gerund. **Estoy escribiendo a mis padres** refers to an action in progress.

Referring to timeless ideas

Creo que es difícil	*I think it's difficult*
El no está de acuerdo	*He doesn't agree*
No me gusta	*I don't like it*

Asking questions regarding present states and events

¿Cómo están tus padres?	*How are your parents?*
(Están bien)	*(They're fine)*
¿Oyes ese ruido?	*Do you hear that noise?*
(No lo oigo)	*(I can't hear it)*
¿En qué piensas?	*What are you thinking about?*
(Estoy preocupado)	*(I'm worried)*

Resumen gramatical

1   3rd conjugation verbs

Verbs whose infinitive ends in **-ir**, for example **vivir** (*to live*) and **escribir** (*to write*), are known as 3rd conjugation verbs. In Unit 7 we studied the present tense of 1st and 2nd conjugation verbs. In this Unit we shall begin by illustrating the present tense forms of regular 3rd conjugation verbs.

vivir (*to live*)			
singular		**plural**	
vivo	*I live*	vivimos	*we live*
vives	*you live* (fam.)	vivís	*you live* (fam.)
vive	*you live* (pol.)	viven	*you live* (pol.)
	he/she/it lives		*they live*

All the examples given below will illustrate the usages already explained and listed under **Objetivos** and **Nota preliminar**.

¿Dónde vives?	*Where do you live?*
Vivo en Londres	*I live in London*
¿Subes?	*Are you going up?*
Subo ahora mismo	*I'm going up right away*
El banco abre a las 3.00	*The bank opens at 3.00*
¿Qué escribes?	*What are you writing?*
Escribo una carta	*I'm writing a letter*

2 Irregular verbs

There are many verbs in Spanish which do not follow a fixed pattern in their conjugation. They are irregular. In the present tense, some verbs are irregular only in the 1st person singular. Here is a list of the most common. Those marked with an asterisk (*) are also stem-changing (see below).

-ar verbs

dar *to give*	doy *I give*

-er verbs

conocer *to know*	conozco *I know*
hacer *to do*	hago *I do, make*
parecer *to appear, seem*	parezco *I appear, seem*
pertenecer *to belong*	pertenezco *I belong*
poner *to put*	pongo *I put*
saber *to know*	sé *I know*
tener* *to have*	tengo *I have*
traer *to bring*	traigo *I bring*
ver *to see*	veo *I see*

-ir verbs

conducir *to drive*	conduzco *I drive*

decir* *to say, tell*		digo *I say, tell*	
oír *to hear*		oigo *I hear*	
salir *to go out*		salgo *I go out*	
venir* *to come*		vengo *I come*	

Nota: oír has other changes: **i** changes to **y** in the 2nd and 3rd person singular and the 3rd person plural:

oigo	oímos
oyes	oís
oye	oyen

Some verbs, for example **ser** (*to be*), **estar** (*to be*), **haber** (*to have*, auxiliary verb) and **ir** (*to go*) are highly irregular. (For the present tense of **ser** see Unit 1, for **estar** Unit 3, for **haber** Unit 19).

Present tense forms of *ir*			
voy	*I go*	vamos	*we go*
vas	*you go* (fam.)	vais	*you go* (fam.)
va	*you go* (pol.)	van	*you go* (pol.)
	he/she/it/goes		*they go*

¿Adónde vas?	*Where are you going?*
Voy al cine	*I'm going to the cinema*
Allí va Manuel	*There goes Manuel*

Nota: For a list of most common irregular verbs in all tenses see pages 221–226 of **Apuntes gramaticales**.

3 Stem-changing verbs

Some verbs undergo a change in the stem (the main part of the verb without its ending) which occurs only when the stem is stressed. Therefore, the 1st and 2nd person plural are not affected by this change. Stem-changing verbs have the same endings as regular verbs.

Here is a list of the most common stem-changing verbs in the present tense.

<table>
<tr><td colspan="4" align="center">Verbs which change e to ie:</td></tr>
<tr><td colspan="2">-ar</td><td colspan="2">-er</td></tr>
<tr><td>cerrar</td><td>to close, shut</td><td>encender</td><td>to light, turn on</td></tr>
<tr><td>despertar(se)</td><td>to wake up</td><td>entender</td><td>to understand</td></tr>
<tr><td>empezar</td><td>to begin</td><td>perder</td><td>to lose</td></tr>
<tr><td>nevar</td><td>to snow</td><td>querer</td><td>to want</td></tr>
<tr><td>pensar</td><td>to think</td><td>tener</td><td>to have</td></tr>
<tr><td colspan="4" align="center">-ir</td></tr>
<tr><td>herirse</td><td>to hurt oneself</td><td>sentir(se)</td><td>to feel</td></tr>
<tr><td>preferir</td><td>to prefer</td><td>venir</td><td>to come</td></tr>
</table>

Here is an example of one of the above verbs in all its forms:

<table>
<tr><td colspan="4" align="center">pensar to think</td></tr>
<tr><td>pienso</td><td>I think</td><td>pensamos</td><td>we think</td></tr>
<tr><td>piensas</td><td>you think (fam.)</td><td>pensáis</td><td>you think (fam.)</td></tr>
<tr><td>piensa</td><td>you think (pol.)
he/she thinks</td><td>piensan</td><td>you think (pol.)
they think</td></tr>
</table>

<table>
<tr><td colspan="4" align="center">Verbs which change o to ue:</td></tr>
<tr><td colspan="2">-ar</td><td colspan="2">-er</td></tr>
<tr><td>acostarse</td><td>to go to bed</td><td>devolver</td><td>to return, give back</td></tr>
<tr><td>acordarse</td><td>to remember</td><td>doler</td><td>to hurt, feel pain</td></tr>
<tr><td>comprobar</td><td>to check</td><td>llover</td><td>to rain</td></tr>
<tr><td>contar</td><td>to tell, count</td><td>moverse</td><td>to move</td></tr>
<tr><td>encontrar</td><td>to find</td><td>poder</td><td>to be able</td></tr>
<tr><td>mostrar</td><td>to show</td><td>soler</td><td>to be accustomed to</td></tr>
<tr><td>recordar</td><td>to remember</td><td>volver</td><td>to return</td></tr>
<tr><td>rogar</td><td>to ask, beg</td><td></td><td></td></tr>
<tr><td colspan="4" align="center">-ir</td></tr>
<tr><td>dormir(se)</td><td>to sleep, go to sleep</td><td>morir(se)</td><td>to die</td></tr>
</table>

Nota: **jugar,** whose stem has a **u**, also changes into **ue**:

juego	*I play*
juegas	*you play* (fam.)
juega	*you play* (pol.) *he/she/it plays*

Here is an example of one of the above verbs in all its forms:

volver *to return*			
vuelvo	*I return*	volvemos	*we return*
vuelves	*you return* (fam.)	volvéis	*you return* (fam.)
vuelve	*you return* (pol.)	vuelven	*you return* (pol.)
	he/she/it returns		*they return*

Verbs which change *e* to *i*:			
conseguir	*to get*	reír(se)	*to laugh*
corregir	*to correct*	repetir	*to repeat*
elegir	*to choose*	seguir	*to follow, continue*
pedir	*to ask (for)*	servir	*to serve*

Notice also the change in the 1st person singular of the following verbs:

conseguir–consigo	elegir–elijo
corregir–corrijo	seguir–sigo

pedir *to ask (for)*			
pido	*I ask*	pedimos	*we ask*
pides	*you ask* (fam.)	pedís	*you ask* (fam.)
pide	*you ask* (pol.)	piden	*you ask* (pol.)
	he/she asks		*they ask*

4 Present continuous (*estar* + gerund)

To refer to events which are actually taking place in the present we can use the present tense or the present continuous (see examples under **Nota preliminar**), which is formed with the verb **estar** followed by a gerund. The forms of the gerund are equivalent to the English **-ing** forms (*working, writing*). In Spanish there are two endings:

-ar verbs form the gerund with **-ando**

(trabajar)	Estoy trabajando	*I'm working*
(estudiar)	Ella está estudiando	*She's studying*

-er and **-ir** verbs form the gerund with **-iendo**

(hacer)	No estoy haciendo nada	*I'm not doing anything*
(escribir)	¿A quién estás escribiendo?	*Who are you writing to?*

Nota: Verbs ending in **-ir** which change the stem from **e** to **i** (see 3 above) also show this change in the gerund.

pedir	pido	pidiendo (*asking*)
repetir	repito	repitiendo (*repeating*)

Verbs which change **e** into **ie** (see 3 above) also take **i** in the gerund. This does not apply to **-ar** and **-er** verbs.

preferir	prefiero	prefiriendo (*preferring*)
sentir	siento	sintiendo (*feeling*)

Verbs ending in **-ir** and certain **-er** verbs which change **o** to **ue** (see 3 above) take **u** in the gerund.

dormir	duermo	durmiendo (*sleeping*)
morir	muero	muriendo (*dying*)
poder	puedo	pudiendo (*being able to*)

Using the present continuous

(*a*)   Although the present tense and the present continuous often overlap in meaning, as in ¿**qué haces**? and ¿**qué estás haciendo**? (*what are you doing?*), the latter construction and not the former is preferred when we want to make it perfectly clear that we are referring to an action which is taking place at the time.

(*b*)   The present continuous is also used in preference to the present when we want to emphasise some kind of change in the action in relation with the past, for example:

¿Qué estás **haciendo** ahora?	*What are you doing now?*
Estoy **viviendo** en California	*I'm living in California*

(*c*)   An action which has been taking place over a period of time in the present is normally expressed through the present continuous.

Estoy **esperando** desde hace dos horas	*I've been waiting for two hours*
Está **lloviendo** desde anoche	*It's been raining since last night*

(*d*)   Disapproval or surprise about an action in progress are often expressed through the present continuous.

¡Pero qué estás diciendo!	*But what are you saying!*
¡Estás leyendo mis cartas!	*You're reading my letters!*

En contexto

1   *Overleaf is an extract from a postcard describing a holiday.*

Querida Carolina,
Te escribo desde Río. Estoy aquí de vacaciones
con mi familia. Hace muchísimo calor y
estamos todos muy morenos. Río es
fantástico. Los chicos están muy contentos.
Ahora están jugando con unos amigos
mientras yo escribo y escucho música brasileña.
¡Qué tranquila estoy! No te imaginas ...

estamos morenos	*we are tanned*
mientras	*while*
escuchar música	*to listen to music*
brasileño/a	*Brazilian*
¡qué tranquila estoy!	*how relaxed I am*
no te imaginas	*you can't imagine*

2 *An appointment with the manager.*

Cliente   Buenos días. Tengo una cita con el gerente. Me llamo
              Hugo Pérez.
Secretaria   Un momento, por favor señor Pérez. El gerente está
              hablando con unos clientes.
Cliente   ¿Y la señora Martínez está?
Secretaria   La señora Martínez ya no trabaja aquí. Está traba-
              jando en una firma en Barcelona. Ah, allí viene el
              gerente ...

tengo una cita	*I have an appointment*
ya no	*not any longer*
el gerente	*manager*

Explicaciones

1 Mientras yo escribo y escucho música *While I write and listen to music*

   The alternative here would be the present continuous: **mientras yo estoy escribiendo y escuchando música.** Notice also **te escribo desde Río** instead of **te estoy escribiendo desde Río**, which is also possible. Where both the present tense and the present continuous are possible, Spanish prefers the use of the present tense.

2 El gerente está hablando con unos clientes *The manager is speaking with some clients*

   The present continuous here puts emphasis on an action in progress.

3 Está trabajando en una firma en Barcelona *She's working for a company in Barcelona*

   This emphasises that there has been a change of action in relation to the past: she used to work here but now she's working in Barcelona.

Expansión

1 Other ways of referring to the present

To refer to events which began at some point in the past but which are still now in progress we can use the following constructions:

Llevar + gerund

El lleva un año viviendo en Francia	*He's been living in France for a year*

Llevamos tres horas espe- rando	*We've been waiting for three hours*
¿Cuánto tiempo llevas tra- bajando aquí?	*How long have you been working here?*

Hace + time phrase + *que* + present tense

Hace una hora que están aquí	*They've been here for an hour*
Hace dos noches que no duermo	*I haven't slept for two nights*

Notice the following alternative to this construction:

Están aquí desde hace una hora	*They've been here for an hour*
No duermo desde hace dos noches	*I haven't slept for two nights*

Observe also the questions:

¿Cuánto tiempo hace que están aquí?	*How long have they been here for?*
¿Cuánto tiempo hace que no duermes?	*How long is it since you slept?*

9 Talking about habitual actions

Nota preliminar

To ask and give information about habitual actions, for instance *Do you get up early?* and *I get up late*, you will need the present tense. Some of the verbs you will encounter in this context correspond to reflexive verbs. These verbs are used with object pronouns such as **me**, **te, se** which are sometimes translated into English as *myself, yourself, himself*, etc. Consider for example

yo me lavo	*I wash (myself)*
él se lava	*he washes (himself)*

To say how often you or others do certain things and to ask similar information of other people you will need the Spanish equivalent of words like *normally* (**normalmente**) *generally* (**generalmente**), etc. These words are known as frequency adverbs. You will also need adverbs to relate a sequence of habitual actions, as in *first I get up, then I wash myself* (**primero me levanto, después me lavo**). These are called adverbs of time.

To ask and state the exact time at which certain habitual actions are performed you will need to use the Spanish equivalent of phrases such as *What time do you go to bed?* (**¿a qué hora te acuestas?**) *I go to bed at 11.00* (**me acuesto a las 11.00**), *What time do you eat?* (**¿a qué hora comes?**), *I eat at 1.00* (**como a la 1.00**).

Have a look at these examples and their English translation before going on to the **Resumen gramatical**.

Asking and giving information about habitual actions

¿Te levantas temprano?	*Do you get up early?*
Me levanto tarde	*I get up late*
¿Qué haces por la noche?	*What do you do in the evening?*
Veo la televisión	*I watch television*
¿Dónde pasa Vd. sus vacaciones?	*Where do you spend your holiday?*
Voy a Londres	*I go to London*

Saying how often you or others do certain things

Vengo aquí de vez en cuando	*I come here from time to time*
Vamos al cine a menudo	*We often go to the cinema*
Nunca llega a la hora	*He/she never arrives on time*

Asking how often other people do certain things

¿Vas a menudo a España?	*Do you go to Spain often?*

¿Vienes siempre en coche?	*Do you always come by car?*
¿Sale Vd. de vacaciones todos los veranos?	*Do you go on holiday every summer?*

Relating a sequence of habitual actions

Primero me levanto, después me lavo, luego desayuno . . .	*First I get up, then I wash (myself), then I have breakfast . . .*
Al llegar a la oficina leo las cartas, después hablo con mi jefe, luego respondo a las cartas más urgentes . . .	*When I arrive at the office I read the mail, then I talk to my boss, later I answer the most urgent letters . . .*

Asking and stating the exact time at which certain actions are performed

¿A qué hora te levantas?	*What time do you get up?*
Me levanto a las 7.30	*I get up at 7.30*
¿A qué hora cenáis?	*What time do you have dinner?*
Cenamos a las 9.00	*We have dinner at 9.00*

Resumen gramatical

1   Reflexive verbs

A reflexive verb is one that is normally indicated by **-se** added to the infinitive, e.g. levantarse (*to get up*), lavarse (*to wash*). **Se** is sometimes translated into English as oneself, e.g., alegrarse (*to enjoy oneself*), but often it is not expressed at all. The reflexive pronouns **me, te, se, nos, os, se**, could be said to correspond to forms such as *myself, yourself, himself, herself*, etc.

Reflexive verbs are conjugated in the usual way but with a reflexive pronoun preceding the conjugated verb. For example:

	levantarse *to get up*		
me levanto	*I get up*	nos levantamos	*we get up*
te levantas	*you get up* (fam.)	os levantáis	*you get up*
se levanta	*you get up* (pol.) *he/she gets up*	se levantan	*you get up* *they get up*

Los sábados siempre me levanto tarde	*On Saturdays I always get up late*
Se levanta y se va al trabajo	*He gets up and goes to work*
Nos levantamos antes de las 6.00	*We get up before 6.00*

Infinitive forms

When there is an infinitive the reflexive pronoun follows the **-ar, -er** or **-ir** and becomes one word with the infinitive.

Después de ducharme desayuno	*After taking a shower I have breakfast*
Antes de acostarse lee un rato	*Before he goes to bed he reads for a while*

Position of the reflexive pronoun

In a construction finite verb (or conjugated verb) + infinitive, the reflexive pronoun may either precede the finite verb or be attached to the infinitive (as above). The latter appears to be more frequent and is probably easier to remember.

Tengo que marcharme	*I have to leave*
Me tengo que marchar	*I have to leave*

Some common reflexive verbs

There is a large number of reflexive verbs in Spanish. Here is a list of some of the most frequent. The (ie), (ue) or (i) next to the verb shows that its stem changes in the present tense (see Unit 8).

acostarse (ue)	*to go to bed*	lavarse	*to wash*
acordarse (ue)	*to remember*	levantarse	*to get up*
		marcharse	*to leave*
afeitarse	*to shave*	morirse (ue)	*to die*
alegrarse	*to be glad*	moverse (ue)	*to move*
bañarse	*to have a bath*	olvidarse	*to forget*
casarse	*to get married*	pararse	*to stop*
cortarse	*to cut oneself*	peinarse	*to comb one's hair*
despertarse (ie)	*to wake up*	probarse (ue)	*to try on*
equivocarse	*to make a mistake*	reírse (i)	*to laugh*
hallarse	*to be (situated)*	sentarse (ie)	*to sit down*
herirse (ie)	*to hurt oneself*	sentirse (ie)	*to feel*

2 Adverbs in *-mente*

In English we often form adverbs by adding *-ly* to an adjective, as in *normally* or *frequently*. In Spanish many adverbs are formed by adding **-mente** to the feminine form of the adjective, for example **rápida** (*rapid*) becomes **rápidamente** (*rapidly*); **lenta** (*slow*) becomes **lentamente** (*slowly*). Notice that if the adjective carries an accent, the accent is kept in the adverb.

If the adjective ends in a consonant, simply add **-mente**. Here are some examples with adverbs which refer to the frequency with which we perform certain actions:

Normal**mente** me acuesto tarde	*I normally go to bed late*
General**mente** no desayuno	*I usually don't have breakfast*
Vienen usual**mente** solos	*They usually come on their own*

Nota: when there are two or more consecutive adverbs in **-mente** joined by a conjunction, e.g., **y** (*and*), **pero** (*but*), only the final one takes the ending **-mente**, for example:

el trabaja rápida y eficiente- *he works rapidly and effi-*
mente *ciently*

3 Frequency adverbs

The following adverbs and adverbial phrases are commonly used to relate the frequency with which one does something.

frecuentemente	*frequently*
generalmente	*generally, usually*
normalmente	*normally*
usualmente	*usually*
a menudo	*often*
a veces	*sometimes*
de vez en cuando	*from time to time*
una vez, dos veces (por semana)	*once, twice (a week)*
siempre	*always*
nunca	*never*
todos los días	*every day*
cada día (semana, mes, año)	*every day (every week, month, year)*

Examples:

Ella nunca sale de noche *She never goes out at night*
Van a Sevilla dos veces al *They go to Seville twice a*
año *year*
La veo a menudo *I see her often*
Nunca me llama *He/she never calls me*
No me llama nunca *He/she never calls me*

Notice the double negative when **nunca** is placed after a verb.

4 Adverbs of time

The following adverbs are commonly used to relate a sequence of habitual actions:

primero	*first, firstly*
después	*afterwards*
entonces	*then*
finalmente	*finally*
posteriormente	*then, later*
antes	*before*

Examples:

Antes de almorzar toma una copa en el bar	*Before having lunch he/she has a drink in the bar*
Después de almorzar toma un café	*After having lunch he/she has a coffee*
Primero saluda a su secretaria y luego entra al despacho	*First he/she says hello to his/her secretary and then he/she goes into the office*

5 Preposition *a* in time phrases

To ask about the exact time at which certain actions are performed we use the phrase **¿a qué hora?** (*at what time?*) followed by the corresponding verb:

¿**a qué hora** empiezas a trabajar?	*What time do you start work?*
¿**A qué hora** sales de la oficina?	*What time do you leave the office?*

In the reply we use the preposition **a** followed by the corresponding time:

Empiezo **a** las 9.00	*I start at 9.00*
Normalmente salgo **a** las 7.00	*I normally leave at 7.00*

En contexto

1 *Read this extract from a letter in which Ignacio, a student, relates his daily activities to a new friend.*

Estudio en un instituto de Granada y tengo
clases de lunes a viernes por la mañana y
por la tarde. Generalmente me levanto a eso
de las 8.00 y me voy al instituto que está
muy cerca de casa. Al mediodía vuelvo a casa
a comer y a las 3.00 regreso al instituto.
A las 6.00 termino las clases y vuelvo
nuevamente a casa. A veces salgo con mis
amigos ...

un instituto	*secondary school*
por la mañana/tarde	*in the morning/afternoon*
a eso de	*around*
me voy (irse)	*I leave (to leave, go)*
al mediodía	*at midday*
comer	*to have lunch* (also *to eat*)
nuevamente	*again*

2 *Alicia talks to a friend about her daily routine at work.*

Cristóbal ¿Qué horario de trabajo tienes?

Alicia Pues, no tengo un horario fijo, pero normalmente llego a la oficina a las 8.00 y estoy allí hasta las 4.00.

Cristóbal	¿Trabajas también los sábados?
Alicia	No, los sábados no trabajo. Generalmente voy con José, mi marido, al supermercado y por la tarde nos quedamos en casa. De vez en cuando cenamos fuera o vamos al cine.
Cristóbal	¿Y los domingos qué hacéis?
Alicia	Bueno, los domingos muchas veces vamos a la sierra. Allí tenemos una casa para pasar los fines de semana . . .

el horario de trabajo	*working hours*
un horario fijo	*fixed working hours*
fuera	*out*
muchas veces	*many times*
la sierra	*mountains*
pasar	*to spend*

Explicaciones

1   A eso de las 8.00   *About 8.00*

Other ways of expressing approximate times are:

> alrededor de las 8.00
> sobre las 8.00
> a las 8.00 aproximadamente

(These all mean *about 8.00*.)

2   Me voy al instituto   *I leave for school*

Here the verb is **irse** (*to leave, go*). **Me voy** (*I'm leaving*) is a complete sentence in itself, whereas **voy** is incomplete:

> voy al instituto   *I go to school*
> voy al cine   *I go to the cinema*

Expansión

1 *Soler* + infinitive

We can also ask and answer questions about habitual actions by using the construction **soler** (o→ue) plus infinitive. **Soler** by itself translates into English as *to be in the habit of, usually . . .*

Examples:

¿Qué **suele** hacer Vd. en el verano?	*What do you usually do in the summer?*
Suelo salir de vacaciones	*I usually go on holiday*
¿Dónde **sueles** comer?	*Where do you normally eat?*
Suelo comer en un restaurante	*I usually eat in a restaurant*
Solemos trabajar hasta muy tarde	*We usually work until very late*

2 *Acostumbrar a* + infinitive

Like **soler** + infinitive, **acostumbrar a** + infinitive translates into English as *to be in the habit of* or *to be accustomed to, usually . . .*

¿Qué **acostumbras** a hacer?	*What do you usually do?*
Acostumbro a leer mucho	*I usually read a lot*
Acostumbramos a quedarnos en casa	*We usually stay at home*
No **acostumbramos** a hacer eso	*We don't usually do that*

10 Stating possibility, capacity and permission

Objetivos

In this Unit you will learn how to:

State possibility or probability • State capacity • Ask questions regarding possibility and capacity • Request, give and deny permission

Contenido gramatical

'Poder' (+infinitive) • 'Saber' (+infinitive) • 'Se' in impersonal sentences • 'Ser' posible + infinitive

Nota preliminar

Possibility, capacity and permission, as in *It may rain, I can't do that, May I come in?*, can all be expressed in Spanish through the verb **poder** (*can, be able to, may*).

Capacity or the ability to do or not to do something, for example *I can't swim* or *I don't know how to swim* may also be stated with **saber** (literally *to know*).

To ask and say whether one is allowed to do something, as in *Can one smoke here?* or *One can't park here*, we use the impersonal word **se**.

Have a look at these examples and their English translation before going on to the **Resumen gramatical**.

Stating possibility or probability

Puede llover	*It may rain*
Puede estar en casa	*He/she may be at home*
Podemos tener éxito	*We may be successful*

Stating capacity

No puedo hacer eso	*I can't do that*
Puedo estar aquí a las 6.00	*I can be here at 6.00*
No sé nadar	*I can't swim (I don't know how to swim)*

Asking questions regarding possibility and capacity

¿Qué puede suceder?	*What can happen?*
¿Puede Vd. volver mañana?	*Can you come back tomorrow?*
¿Sabcs jugar al tenis?	*Do you know how to play tennis?*

Requesting, giving and denying permission

¿Puedo fumar?	*May I smoke?*
Aquí no se puede fumar	*You can't smoke here*
¿Se puede aparcar aquí?	*Can one park here?*
Sí, se puede	*Yes, it is allowed* (literally one can)

Resumen gramatical

1   *Poder* (+infinitive) (can, be able to, may)

Poder, a verb whose stem changes from **o** to **ue** in the present tense (**puedo, puedes, puede, podemos, podéis, pueden**), is normally used with an infinitive to express possibility, capacity or permission. Here are some further examples:

Puede suceder	*It may happen* (possibility)
No **puedo** ayudarte	*I can't help you* (capacity)
¿**Puedo** pasar?	*May I come in?* (permission)

2   *Saber* (+ infinitive) (to be able to)

Saber (literally *to know*) is often used to express capacity or ability. Here are some further examples:

No **sé** cocinar	*I don't know how to cook*
Ella no **sabe** bailar	*She doesn't know how to dance*
¿**Sabes** tocar el piano?	*Do you know how to play the piano?*

3   *Se* in impersonal sentences

Impersonal sentences such as *Is it possible to go in? Can one eat here?* and *One can't listen to music here*, are expressed in Spanish through the word **se** followed by **poder** in the 3rd person singular plus an infinitive. Look at these examples:

¿**Se puede** entrar?	*Is it possible to go in?/can one go in?*
¿**Se puede** comer aquí?	*Can one eat here?*
Aquí no **se puede** escuchar música	*One can't listen to music here*

Nota: more on the use of **se** in Unit 11.

En contexto

1 *Where can we park?*

Conductor	Perdone, ¿se puede aparcar aquí?
Policía	No señor, aquí no se puede.
Conductor	¿Dónde se puede aparcar?
Policía	En la plaza Mayor, al final de la calle.
Conductor	¿Puedo doblar aquí?
Policía	Aquí no, pero puede doblar en la próxima calle a la derecha y luego bajar hasta la plaza.
Conductor	Gracias.
Policía	De nada.

doblar	*to turn*
bajar	*to go down*
hasta	*as far as, to*

2 *What can one do in Barcelona?*

Turista A	¿Qué se puede hacer en Barcelona?
Turista B	Se puede ir a algún museo, al museo de Picasso por ejemplo. También se puede visitar el Barrio Gótico, que es muy bonito. Puede ir al puerto, que está muy cerca de aquí . . .
Turista A	¿Y por la noche qué se puede hacer?
Turista B	Por la noche puede Vd. ir a algún espectáculo, al teatro o a la ópera por ejemplo, o tomar una copa en un bar . . .
Turista A	Y los fines de semana, ¿dónde puedo ir?
Turista B	Puede ir a la playa. Sitges no está muy lejos. Se puede ir en tren o en coche . . .

el puerto	*port*
el espectáculo	*entertainment, show*
la playa	*beach*

Explicaciones

¿Qué se puede hacer en Barcelona?	*What can one do in Barcelona?*
Se puede ir a algún museo	*One can go to a museum*

Notice that an alternative translation for **se** in these sentences and other sentences from the dialogues would be *you: what can **you** do in Barcelona? **You** can go to a museum.*

Expansión

Ser posible + infinitive

Possibility may also be expressed in Spanish with the phrase **es posible** plus infinitive, a construction which is much less frequent in Spanish than its English equivalent: *it's possible.*

¿Es posible hablar con el señor Díaz?	*Is it possible to speak to señor Díaz?*
Lo siento, no **es posible**	*I'm sorry, it isn't possible*
¿Es posible reservar una habitación por teléfono?	*Is it possible to book a room on the phone?*
Por supuesto que **es posible**	*Of course it's possible*

Nota: For other ways of expressing possibility and probability refer to Unit 23.

11 Describing processes and procedures

Objetivos

In this Unit you will learn how to:

Describe processes and procedures • Ask questions regarding processes and procedures

Contenido gramatical

Passive and active sentences • Passive sentences with 'ser' + past participle • Passive sentences with 'se' • Impersonal 'tú' • Impersonal 'ellos'

Nota preliminar

To describe the various steps in a process as in: *The oranges are cut and then they are taken to the market where they are sold directly to the public*, we can use a passive sentence with **ser** (*to be*) followed by a past participle, which is a direct translation of the English *they are cut, they are taken, they are sold*: **las naranjas son cortadas y después son llevadas al mercado donde son vendidas directamente al público.** An alternative is to use a passive construction with **se**, similar to that which we studied in Unit 10: **las naranjas se cortan y después se llevan al mercado donde se venden directamente al público.**

In the grammar section below you will find a more detailed analysis of the uses of these two constructions, with particular reference to the description of processes and procedures.

Have a look at these examples and their English translation before going on to the **Resumen gramatical**.

Describing processes and procedures

Las cebollas se cortan en trozos pequeños y luego se fríen durante cinco minutos . . .

The onions are cut into small pieces and then they are fried for five minutes . . .

La fruta es puesta en cajas y es llevada a los puertos desde donde es enviada a distintos países de Europa . . .

The fruit is put into cases and it's taken to the ports from where it's sent to different European countries . . .

Asking questions regarding processes and procedures

¿Cómo se prepara una tortilla a la española?

How do you make a Spanish omelette?

¿Cómo se obtiene un permiso de trabajo?

How do you get a work permit?

¿Como se consigue un visado de turista?

How do you get a tourist visa?

Resumen gramatical

1 Passive and active sentences

Look at these sentences in English:

The farmers cut the oranges.

The oranges are cut by the farmers.

The first is an active sentence with an active verb: *the farmers cut the oranges*. The second sentence is passive: *the oranges are cut by the farmers*. In the passive sentence *the oranges* is the subject and *the farmers* is the agent carrying out the action expressed by the verb. In Spanish there are also active and passive sentences:

Los campesinos **cortan** las naranjas (active)	*The farmers cut the oranges*
Las naranjas **son cortadas por** los campesinos (passive)	*The oranges are cut by the farmers*

2 Passive sentences with *ser* + past participle

There are two main ways of forming passive sentences in Spanish. As in the sentence above, we may use the verb **ser** plus a past participle. The past participle is formed by adding the ending **-ado** to the stem of **-ar** verbs and **-ido** to the stem of **-er** and **-ir** verbs, for example:

cortar	Es cortado	*It's cut*
vender	Es vendido	*It's sold*
expedir	Es expedido	*It's despatched*

In this construction, the past participle will change for gender and number:

Las naranjas son cortadas	*The oranges are cut*
La fruta es vendida	*Fruit is sold*
Los productos son expedidos	*Products are despatched*

Irregular past participles

Some past participles are irregular. Here is a list of the most common ones:

abrir	(*to open*)	abierto
decir	(*to say, tell*)	dicho
escribir	(*to write*)	escrito
hacer	(*to do, make*)	hecho
poner	(*to put*)	puesto
romper	(*to break*)	roto
ver	(*to see*)	visto
volver	(*to come back*)	vuelto

Using passive sentences with *ser*

You should bear in mind the following points when using passive sentences with *ser*:

- The passive with **ser** is found more frequently in written and more formal language.
- The passive with **ser** is extremely uncommon in the spoken language, particularly in Spain.
- If the agent of the action expressed by the verb is mentioned, use a passive with **ser** and not with **se**, e.g. las naranjas **son** cortadas por las campesinos.
- Some verbs do not allow the use of the passive with **ser** but, as there is no rule about it, only usage will tell you which ones cannot be used.

3   Passive sentences with *se*

In Unit 10 we studied the use of **se** with a 3rd person verb in impersonal sentences, e.g.

aquí no **se** puede aparcar   *one can't park here*

The same construction – **se** plus 3rd person verb – is used with a passive meaning, for example:

Primero se hierve el agua,
  después se calienta la tetera con un poco de agua,
  se tira el agua y se pone
  una cucharadita de té por
  persona . . .

First you boil the water, then
  you heat the teapot with
  some water, you throw
  away that water and you
  put in one teaspoonful of
  tea per person . . .

Using passive sentences with *se*

You should bear in mind the following points when using passive sentences with **se**:

• The verb agrees in number (singular or plural) with the subject:

Se fabrica aquí   *It's manufactured here*
Se fabrican aquí   *They're manufactured here*

Se produce en España   *It's produced in Spain*
Se producen en España   *They're produced in Spain*

• Passive sentences with **se** are not used when the agent of the action expressed by the verb is present. In such cases we must use a passive with **ser**:

Los viajeros **son** recibidos   *Travellers are received by a*
  por un guía . . .   *guide . . .*

• Generally speaking, passive sentences with **se** are more frequent than those with **ser**.

En contexto

1 *Read these instructions on how to get a visa for a South American country.*

Para obtener un visado de estudiante se debe ir personalmente al Consulado donde se rellena un formulario con los datos personales y los motivos del viaje. Se deben llevar tres fotografías tamaño pasaporte y una carta de la institución donde se va a estudiar. El visado debe ser solicitado por lo menos un mes antes de la fecha en que se piensa viajar. Para más información se puede llamar al teléfono 396 6907.

el consulado	*consulate*
los datos personales	*personal information*
los motivos	*reasons*
el viaje	*travel*
tamaño pasaporte	*passport size*
debe ser solicitado	*it must be requested*
por lo menos	*at least*
la fecha	*date*
en que se piensa viajar	*when you're thinking of travelling*

2 *Read this extract from a tourist brochure.*

Los viajeros son recibidos en el aeropuerto por un guía y desde allí son trasladados a sus respectivos hoteles donde son atendidos por nuestro propio personal. Las excursiones son organizadas por agencias locales y se pueden pagar en moneda extranjera o moneda local . . .

son recibidos	*they're met*
son trasladados	*they're transferred*
son atendidos	*they're looked after*
se pueden pagar	*they ean be paid for*
en moneda extranjera	*in foreign currency*

Explicaciones

1 Notice the agreement in number between verb and subject in the following sentences with **se**:

Se rellena un formulario	*A form is filled in*
Se deben llevar tres fotogra-fías	*Three photographs must be taken*

2 Notice the agreement in number and gender between verb and subject in the following sentences with **ser**:

Los viajeros **son** recibid**os** . . .	*Travellers are met . . .*
Las excursiones **son** organi-zad**as** . . .	*Excursions are organised . . .*

Expansión

1 Impersonal *tú* (you)

Processes may also be described using **tú** in an impersonal way:

Primero cortas la cebolla, luego la fríes . . .	*First you cut the onion, then you fry it . . .*
Primero rellenas este formu-lario y lo llevas al Consu-lado . . .	*First you fill in this form and you take it to the Consu-late . . .*

2 Impersonal *ellos* (they)

In colloquial speech the passive is often replaced by the impersonal **ellos**:

Reciben a los turistas en el aeropuerto y los trasladan a sus respectivos hoteles . . .	*They meet the tourists at the airport and they take them to their hotels . . .*

12 Expressing wants and preferences

Objetivos

In this Unit you will learn how to:

Ask and answer questions about wants • Ask and answer questions about preferences

---

Contenido gramatical

'Querer' + noun/pronoun/verb • 'Preferir' + noun/pronoun/verb • Direct object pronouns • Personal 'a' • Other verbs expressing wants

---

Nota preliminar

To ask and answer questions about wants, for example *What do you want?*, *I want some apples, I want these ones, I want to buy some apples*, we use **querer** (e→ie).

To ask and answer questions about preferences, as in *Which one do you prefer?*, *I prefer this room, I prefer this one, I prefer to take this room*, we use **preferir** (e→ie).

To say what you want or prefer you may also need pronouns, that is, words like *it*, *them*, as in *I don't want it, Do you want them?* These are called direct object pronouns.

These and other points in relation to the expression of wants and preferences are explained in the grammar section below.

Have a look at these examples and their English translation before going on to the **Resumen gramatical**.

Asking and answering questions about wants

¿Qué quieres?	*What do you want?*
Quiero manzanas	*I want some apples*
Quiero éstas	*I want these ones*
Quiero comprar manzanas	*I want to buy some apples*

Asking and answering questions about preferences

¿Cuál prefiere Vd.?	*Which one do you prefer?*
Prefiero esta habitación	*I prefer this room*
Prefiero ésta	*I prefer this one*
Prefiero tomar esta habitación	*I prefer to take this room*

Resumen gramatical

1   *Querer* + noun/pronoun/verb

Querer (e→ie) is the verb most frequently used in Spanish to ask and answer questions about wants. It may be followed by:

A noun

Quiero **un zumo de naranja**	*I want an orange juice*
Quiero **un bolígrafo**	*I want a ball point pen*
Queremos **una habitación**	*We want a room*
Quieren **un coche**	*They want a car*

A pronoun

Quiero pollo. ¿Cómo lo quiere? Lo quiero asado	*I want chicken. How do you want it? I want it roasted*
Quiero chuletas de cerdo. ¿Con qué las quiere? Las quiero con ensalada	*I want pork chops. What do you want them with? I want them with salad*
Quiero esto	*I want this*

A verb

Quiero alquilar un coche	*I want to hire a car*
Queremos ir al teatro	*We want to go to the theatre*
Ella quiere descansar	*She wants to rest*
¿Qué quieres hacer?	*What do you want to do?*

2   *Preferir* + noun/pronoun/verb

Preferir (e→ie) is the verb most frequently used in Spanish to ask and answer questions about preferences. It may be followed by:

A noun

Prefiero el tenis	*I prefer tennis*
Él prefiere el fútbol	*He prefers football*
¿Qué prefieres?	*What do you prefer*
Prefiero la playa	*I prefer the beach*

A pronoun

Prefiero éste	*I prefer this one*
Prefiero pescado. ¿Cómo lo prefiere? Lo prefiero a la plancha	*I prefer fish. How do you prefer it? I prefer it grilled*

A verb

Preferimos **ir** a Mallorca	*We prefer to go to Mallorca*
Prefieren **quedarse** en casa	*They prefer to stay at home*
Luis prefiere **aprender** inglés	*Luis prefers to learn English*

3 Direct object pronouns

1st and 2nd person:

Words such as *me, you, him, her, it,* etc., as in *He prefers me, I prefer you* and *I don't want it*, are called direct object pronouns. Object pronouns for the 1st and 2nd person singular are:

Singular			
me	*me*	Me prefiere	*He prefers me*
te	*you* (fam.)	Te prefiere	*He prefers you*
Plural			
nos	*us*	Nos prefiere	*He prefers us*
os	*you* (fam.)	Os prefiere	*He prefers you*

3rd person:

Now look at these examples and explanations regarding the use of 3rd person object pronouns.

¿Cómo quiere el pescado?	*How do you want the fish?*
Lo quiero frito	*I want it fried*
¿Cómo quiere las patatas?	*How do you want the potatoes?*
Las quiero fritas	*I want them fried*

In order to avoid the repetition of the nouns **el pescado** and **las patatas** we have used instead the pronouns **lo** (masculine, singular) and **las** (feminine, plural). **Lo** and **las** are direct object pronouns. **Lo** refers back to the object **el pescado** and **las** refers back to **las patatas**. Direct object pronouns agree in gender and number with the noun they refer to. Here are the 3rd person forms:

lo (masc. sing.)	**los** (masc. pl.)
la (fem. sing.)	**las** (fem. pl.)

Direct object pronouns can refer to people

In the following sentences 3rd person object pronouns refer to people rather than things:

Prefiero a Carmen	*I prefer Carmen*
La prefiero	*I prefer her*
Prefiero a Carmen y Elena	*I prefer Carmen and Elena*
Las prefiero	*I prefer them*

Carmen, in the first sentence, and Carmen and Elena in the second sentence, are direct objects replaced by **la** (fem. sing.) and **las** (fem. pl.) respectively. The use of **la** and **las** for a human female direct object seems to present no variation throughout the Spanish speaking world. However, when it comes to human male direct objects there are two main dialectal differences.

¿Le **or** *lo?*

In the Spanish speaking countries of Latin America as well as in some parts of non-central Spain you will hear **lo** (singular) and **los** (plural) used for males, as for things. In Madrid and in some regions of central Spain in general, you are much more likely to hear **le** (singular) and **les** (plural) used for human males and **lo** (singular) and **los** (plural) used for things. Both usages are correct but the latter may be easier for you to remember. Here are some examples:

Yo **lo** prefiero	*I prefer him/it*
Yo **le** prefiero	*I prefer him*
Ella **lo** quiere	*She loves him/it*
Ella **le** quiere	*She loves him*

Direct address

In direct address **le (lo)** – **la** and **les (los)** – **las** stand for **usted** and **ustedes** respectively, for example

Ellos **le (lo)** prefieren   *They prefer you* (masc. sing.)
Yo **la** quiero aquí   *I want you here* (fem. sing.)

Position of direct object pronouns

The normal position of the object pronoun is before the finite (or conjugated) verb, as shown in the examples above. However, in phrases where a finite verb precedes an infinitive, the object pronoun may either precede the finite verb or be attached to the infinitive.

Quiero hacer**lo**   *I want to do it*
Lo quiero hacer   *I want to do it*

4   Personal *a*

Observe these sentences:

Prefiero **a** Carmen   *I prefer Carmen*
Quiero **a** Juan   *I love Juan*

A peculiarity of Spanish is that the preposition **a** is placed before a direct object if the object is a definite person. This use of the preposition **a** is known as 'personal **a**'.

En contexto

1   *In a restaurant.*

Humberto   La carta, por favor.
Camarero   Aquí la tiene señor.
Humberto   Gracias.

(Humberto and his friend call the waiter and order their meal)

Humberto	Yo quiero sopa de verduras y de segundo pescado con ensalada.
Camarero	El pescado, ¿cómo lo quiere? Frito, a la plancha . . .
Humberto	Lo prefiero a la plancha.
Camarero	¿Y usted señor?
Juan	Para mí una tortilla de patatas y de segundo quiero chuletas de cerdo.
Camarero	Las chuletas, ¿con qué las quiere?
Juan	Con puré.
Camarero	¿Y para beber?
Humberto	Una botella de vino de la casa.
Camarero	¿Prefieren blanco o tinto?
Humberto	Tinto.
Camarero	De acuerdo, un momento, por favor.

la carta	*menu*
la sopa de verduras	*vegetable soup*
de segundo	*as a second course*
una botella	*a bottle*
el vino de la casa	*house wine*
blanco o tinto	*white or red*
de acuerdo	*all right*

2 *Buying a shirt.*

Dependienta	Buenas tardes. ¿Qué desea señorita?
Elisa	Quiero una camisa de ésas. ¿Cuánto valen?
Dependienta	Éstas las tenemos en oferta a 3500 pesetas. ¿De qué color la quiere?
Elisa	La prefiero en azul.
Dependienta	¿Y de qué talla?
Elisa	De la talla 38.
Dependienta	Aquí tiene Vd. una en azul.
Elisa	Sí, está muy bien. ¿Puedo probármela?
Dependienta	Sí, cómo no. Pase por aquí, por favor.

¿qué desea?	what would you like?
una camisa	shirt
¿cuánto valen?	how much are they?
en oferta	special offer
¿de qué color?	what colour?
¿de qué talla?	what size?
¿puedo probármela?	may I try it on?
cómo no	certainly
pase por aquí	come this way

Explicaciones

1 Notice the use of direct object pronouns in the following sentences from dialogue 1:

Aquí la tiene. La refers back to **la carta.**
El pescado, ¿cómo lo quiere? Lo refers back to **el pescado.**
Las chuletas, ¿con qué las quiere? Las refers back to **las chuletas.**

2 ¿Puedo probármela? *May I try it on?*

The verb here is **probarse** (*to try on*), a reflexive verb. Both the reflexive pronoun **me** and the direct object pronoun **la** (which refers back to **la camisa**) have been added to the infinitive. An alternative position would be: ¿**me la** puedo probar?

Expansión

Other verbs expressing wants

1 *Desear*

Desear, a regular verb, literally means *to wish*. It is normally used in more formal contexts and is generally much less frequent than **querer**.

¿**Desea** Vd. pasar?	*Do you wish to come in?*
Deseo estar solo	*I wish to be alone*
¿Qué **desea?**	*What would you like?* (in a shop or office)

2   *Quisiera*

Quisiera, which corresponds to the 1st person singular of the imperfect subjunctive (see Unit 22) is often used to express wants in more formal situations:

Quisiera una habitación	*I'd like a room*
Quisiera hablar con Vd.	*I'd like to speak to you*

You may also hear the 3rd person singular and 1st person plural:

El **quisiera** ayudar	*He'd like to help*
Quisiéramos hacer algo	*We'd like to do something*

Note that the 1st and 3rd person singular share the same form.

13 Expressing likes and dislikes

Objetivos

In this Unit you will learn how to:

Say whether you like or dislike something • Give similar information about other people • Ask questions about likes and dislikes

---

Contenido gramatical

'Gustar' • Indirect object pronouns • Prepositional forms of pronouns • Position of indirect object pronouns • Other verbs expressing likes and dislikes

---

Nota preliminar

To say whether we like or dislike something, as in *I like it* and *we like them*, we normally use the verb **gustar** (*to like*). **Gustar** is a special kind of verb which is used with a set of pronouns called indirect object pronouns, e.g. **me gusta** (*I like it*), **te gusta** (*you like it*, fam.). For emphasis, a further set of pronouns is used in a construction which carries the preposition **a**, e.g., **a mí me gusta** (*I like it*), **a ti te gusta** (*you like it*, fam.). In the grammar section below you will find information about how to use the verb **gustar**, as well as a detailed explanation of the pronouns which are normally used with this verb.

Have a look at these examples and their English translation before going on to the **Resumen gramatical**.

Saying whether you like or dislike something

Me gusta el tenis	*I like tennis*
Me gusta jugar al tenis	*I like to play tennis*
No me gusta el fútbol	*I don't like football*
Nos gusta la natación	*We like swimming*
Nos gusta nadar	*We like to swim*

Saying whether others like or dislike something

Le gusta el campo	*You like* (pol)/*he/she likes the countryside*
A Rosario le gusta la sierra	*Rosario likes the mountains*
A Ernesto le gustan los deportes	*Ernesto likes sports*
A ellos no les gustan las excursiones	*They don't like excursions*

Asking questions about likes and dislikes

¿Te gusta esquiar?	*Do you like skiing?* (fam.)
¿Le gusta a Vd. España?	*Do you like Spain?* (pol.)
¿Os gustan las playas españolas?	*Do you like Spanish beaches?* (fam., pl.)

Resumen gramatical

1   *Gustar*

To say whether we like or dislike something we can use the verb **gustar**. It is a special kind of verb which is normally used in the 3rd person singular or plural, depending on the number of the noun which follows. The verb must be preceded by an indirect object pronoun. These are words such as **me** (*me, to me*), **te** (*you, to you*), as in **me gusta** (*I like it* or, literally, *it is pleasing to me*), **te gusta** (*you like it* or, literally, *it is pleasing to you*). An explanation about indirect object pronouns is necessary before giving further examples of the use of **gustar**.

2 Indirect object pronouns

In Unit 12 we studied direct object pronouns, as found in sentences like **lo quiero** (*I want it*), **los quiero** (*I want them*), **me prefiere** (*he/she prefers me*). Here we are dealing with another set of pronouns – indirect object pronouns – which, although mostly similar in form to the others, are used differently.

1st and 2nd person indirect object pronouns

Consider this sentence:

> El recepcionista me cambia   *The receptionist changes the*
>   el dinero   *money for me*

Here, the subject of the sentence is **el recepcionista** (*the receptionist*), the direct object is **el dinero** (*the money*, the thing changed) and the indirect object is **me** (*for me*, that is, the person for whom the money is changed). First and second person indirect object pronouns are no different in form from direct object pronouns (see page 107). Here are their forms:

Subject pronouns		Indirect object pronouns	
yo	*I*	me	*me, to me, for me*
tú	*you* (fam. sing.)	te	*you, to you, for you*
nosotros	*we*	nos	*us, to us, for us*
vosotros	*you* (pol. pl.)	os	*you, to you, for you*

In sentences with **gustar**, indirect pronouns will translate literally as *to me, to you, to us*:

me gusta	(lit. *it is pleasing to me/I like it*)
te gusta	(lit. *it is pleasing to you/you like it*)
nos gusta	(lit. *it is pleasing to us/we like it*)
os gusta	(lit. *it is pleasing to you/you like it*)

The verb itself may be in the plural:

me gustan	(lit. *they're pleasing to me/I like them*)
te gustan	(lit. *they're pleasing to you/you like them*)
No nos gustan	(lit. *they're not pleasing to us/we don't like them*)

Notice that negative sentences are formed by placing **no** before the pronoun.

Here are some examples of the use of indirect object pronouns with verbs other than **gustar**:

Me/nos da el dinero, por favor	*Will you give me/us the money, please*
¿Te traigo el periódico?	*Shall I bring you the newspaper?*
El me/nos enseña español	*He teaches me/us Spanish*

3rd person indirect object pronouns

In the 3rd person, the indirect object pronoun is **le** for both masculine and feminine. The plural form is **les**:

Subject pronouns		Indirect object pronouns	
usted	*you* (pol.)	le	*you, to you, for you*
él	*he*	le	*him, to him, for him*
ella	*she*	le	*her, to her, for her*
ustedes	*you* (pol.)	les	*you, to you, for you*
ellos/as	*they*	les	*them, to them, for them*

Here are some examples with **gustar**:

Le gusta viajar	*You like/he/she likes to travel*
Les gusta España	*You/they like Spain*
¿**Le** gusta el vino español?	*Do you/does he/she like Spanish wine?*

Here are some examples with verbs other than **gustar**:

¿**Le** doy el pasaporte?	*Shall I give you/him/her the passport?*
Ella **le** prepara la cena	*She prepares dinner for you/him/her*
El **les** repara el coche	*He repairs the car for you/them*

3 Prepositional forms of pronouns

Consider this sentence from the examples above: **Le gusta viajar**. This sentence translates into English in three different ways: *You like to travel, he likes to travel, she likes to travel.* To avoid this kind of ambiguity, and also to emphasise, we use another set of pronouns preceded by the preposition **a**:

A usted le gusta viajar	*You like to travel*
A él le gusta viajar	*He likes to travel*
A ella le gusta viajar	*She likes to travel*

For the plural we use **a ustedes, a ellos, a ellas**:

A ustedes les gusta España	*You like Spain*
A ellos les gusta Madrid	*They like Madrid* (masc.)
A ellas les gusta Sevilla	*They like Seville* (fem.)

Notice also:

A Alfonso no le gusta fumar	*Alfonso does't like to smoke*

A **Cristina** no le gusta beber	*Christina does't like to drink*
A **Luis y Juan** no les gusta esto	*Luis and Juan don't like this*

Emphatic use of prepositional pronouns

Sometimes the function of prepositional pronouns is purely emphatic:

A **mí** me gusta	*I like it*
A **ti** te gusta	*you like it*
A **nosotros** nos gusta	*we like it*
A **vosotros** os gusta	*you like it*

4   Position of indirect object pronouns

The position of indirect object pronouns is the same as that of direct object pronouns, that is, normally before the finite (or conjugated) verb. But when there are two object pronouns in a sentence (which may happen with verbs other than **gustar**), one indirect and one direct, the indirect object pronoun must come first. Consider these sentences:

El me cambia el dinero	*He changes the money for me*
El me lo cambia	*He changes it for me*

When the indirect object **le** or **les** precedes **lo, la, los** or **las,** the indirect object becomes **se:**

Yo **le** cambio el dinero	*I change the money for you*
Yo **lo** cambio	*I change it*
Yo **se** lo cambio	*I change it for you*

En contexto

1   *In Seville for the first time.*

Ella   ¿Te gusta Sevilla?

El   Sí, me gusta muchísimo. ¿Y a ti?
Ella   A mí también, pero hace mucho calor, ¿verdad?
El   Sí, yo prefiero el clima de Galicia.
Ella   A mí no me gusta nada la lluvia. En Galicia llueve
           demasiado.

la lluvia	*rain*
llueve demasiado	*it rains too much*

2 *An interview about Madrid.*

Periodista   Señor, ¿Le gusta a Vd. Madrid?
Señor   Sí y no.
Periodista   ¿Qué es lo que le gusta de Madrid?
Señor   Me gustan sus museos, sus espectáculos, sus
                 restaurantes que son estupendos . . .
Periodista   ¿Y qué es lo que no le gusta?
Señor   Bueno, no me gusta el tráfico excesivo que tiene
                 Madrid. Es una ciudad muy ruidosa y a mí me gusta
                 la tranquilidad.

¿qué es lo que le gusta . . . ?	*what is it you like . . . ?*
ruidoso/a	*noisy*
la tranquilidad	*peace and quiet*

Explicaciones

1 To avoid repetition of the same verb, in this case **gustar**, we use the
construction **a** + prepositional pronoun. Observe these phrases
from dialogue 1 above:

Sí, me gusta muchísimo. ¿Y **a ti**?	*Yes, I like it very much. Do you?*
A mí también	*So do I*

The same construction may be used in negative sentences with **tampoco**:

No me gusta Madrid. ¿Y a usted?	*I don't like Madrid. Do you?*
A mí **tampoco**	*Neither do I*

Expansión

Other verbs expressing likes and dislikes

1   *Encantar* **(to like very much, to love)**

Encantar is used in the same way as **gustar**, but unlike **gustar** it cannot be used in negative sentences:

Me **encanta** la Costa del Sol	*I love the Costa del Sol*
Me **encanta** tomar el sol	*I love to sunbathe*
Nos **encanta** este restaurante	*We love this restaurant*
Nos **encantan** los españoles	*We love Spaniards*
A ella le **encanta** nadar	*She loves swimming*

2   *Agradar* **(to like)**

Agradar is less frequent than **gustar** and it tends to be used in more formal language. It is used in the same way as **gustar** in positive, negative and interrogative sentences.

¿Les **agrada** a Vds. esta ciudad?	*Do you like this city?*
Nos **agrada** mucho	*We like it very much*
No nos **agrada**	*We don't like it*
No me **agrada** tener que hacer eso	*I don't like to have to do that*

14   Asking and giving opinions

Objetivos

In this Unit you will learn how to:
Ask opinions • Give opinions

Contenido gramatical

'Parecer' • Relative pronoun 'que' • Other verbs used in expressing opinions • Phrases expressing opinions

Nota preliminar

The aim of the Unit is to teach you how to ask people what they think about something or somebody and to give opinions with regard to what you or others think. In Spanish, as in English, there are several ways of expressing opinions. Consider for instance the following questions and answers: *What do you think about John?*, *I think he's very nice*, *What's your opinion of this?* and *It seems right*. The examples below will illustrate the most frequent ways of expressing these ideas in Spanish. All the explanations regarding structures and usage will be found in the grammar section.

Have a look at these examples and their English translation before going on to the **Resumen gramatical**.

Asking and giving opinions

¿Qué te parece John?	*What do you think about John?*
Me parece muy simpático	*I think he's very nice (literally, he seems very nice to me)*
¿Qué opinas de esto?	*What's your opinion of this?*
Creo que está bien	*It seems right/I think it's right*
¿Qué piensas de Gloria?	*What do you think about Gloria?*
La considero inteligente	*I consider her bright*
¿Crees que debemos hacerlo?	*Do you think we should do it?*
Creo que sí	*I think so*
Creo que no	*I don't think so*

Resumen gramatical

1   *Parecer* (to think, seem)

To ask and give opinions we can use **parecer**, a 2nd conjugation verb which in this context functions grammatically like **gustar**, that is, it is used in the 3rd person singular or plural and it is preceded by an indirect object pronoun:

¿Qué te **parece** San Sebastián?	*What do you think of San Sebastian?*
Me **parece** una ciudad muy bonita	*I think it's a very nice city*

Nota: Literally, the two sentences above would translate as: *What does San Sebastian seem to you? It seems a very nice city to me.* Likewise:

| ¿Qué os **parecen** estas playas? | *What do you think of these beaches?* (*What do these beaches seem to you?*) |
| Nos **parecen** muy contaminadas | *We think they're very polluted* (*They seem very polluted to us*) |

2 Relative pronoun *que*

Consider these two sentences:

| ¿Te parece **que** él puede hacerlo? | *Do you think he can do it?* |
| Me parece **que** es difícil | *I think it's difficult* |

These sentences carry two clauses, a main clause – **¿te parece?, me parece** – and a relative clause – **que él puede hacerlo, que es difícil** – linked to the main clause by the relative pronoun **que**. **Que** is equivalent in this context to the English word *that*, but unlike English, Spanish cannot omit the relative pronoun. Here are some other examples of the use of the relative pronoun **que** in the context of opinions:

Nos parece **que** es mejor	*We think (that) it's better*
Creo **que** no es conveniente	*I don't think (that) it's convenient*
Él piensa **que** no puede hacerlo	*He thinks (that) he can't do it*
Ellos consideran **que** está incorrecto	*They consider (that) it's incorrect*

Nota: More on relative pronouns on page 218 of **Apuntes gramaticales**.

3 Other verbs used in the expression of opinions

Here are some other verbs used in the expression of opinions:

pensar (e→ie) *to think*

¿Qué **piensa** Vd. de mí?	*What do you think of me?*
Pienso que es Vd. muy amable	*I think you're very kind*
¿Qué **pensáis** vosotros de mi idea?	*What do you think of my idea?*
Pensamos que es una idea excelente	*We think it's an excellent idea*

creer *to think*

¿Qué **cree** Vd. que puede pasar?	*What do you think can happen?*
Creo que no hay que pre-ocuparse	*I don't think one needs to worry*
¿**Crees** tú que es caro?	*Do you think it's expensive?*
Creo que sí	*I think so*
Creo que no	*I don't think so*

opinar *to think*

¿Qué **opinan** Vds. de lo que digo?	*What do you think of what I'm saying?*
Opinamos que Vd. está equi-vocado	*We think you're wrong*
Yo **opino** que Vd. tiene razón	*I think you're right*

considerar *to consider, think*

Considero que debemos ha-blar con él	*I think we should speak to him*
Consideramos que es un tonto	*We think he's a fool*

Ella **considera** que es suficiente

She thinks it's enough

En contexto

1 *Javier and Eva have just met at the lounge of their hotel in Spain.
They discuss the place where they're staying.*

Javier	¿Qué te parece el hotel?
Eva	Creo que no está nada mal, aunque la comida no me parece muy buena.
Javier	Las habitaciones son estupendas, ¿no crees tú?
Eva	Bueno, sí, la mía tiene una vista fantástica, pero es un poco ruidosa, ¿Y la ciudad te gusta?
Javier	Sí, pienso que está bien, pero hay demasiada gente. Prefiero los lugares pequeños.
Eva	Sí, yo también.
Javier	¿Estás libre ahora?
Eva	Sí. No tengo nada que hacer.
Javier	¿Qué te parece si vamos a tomar un café?
Eva	De acuerdo. Vamos.

no está nada mal	*it's not bad at all*
una vista	*a view*
el lugar	*place*
no tengo nada que hacer	*I have nothing to do*
¿qué te parece si vamos . . . ?	*what about going . . . ?*
vamos	*let's go*

Explicaciones

Notice the use of the word **aunque** (*although*) in the following sentence
from the dialogue:

Creo que no está nada mal, **aunque** la comida no me parece muy buena	*I don't think it's bad at all, although I don't think the food is very good*

Aunque is normally used when we wish to establish a contrast between two ideas. Here are some other examples:

Aunque no tengo mucho dinero quiero ir de vacaciones	*Although I don't have much money I want to go on holiday*
José va siempre a Londres, **aunque** no sabe nada de inglés	*José always goes to London, although he doesn't know any English*
Es simpática, **aunque** me parece que es un poco tímida	*She's nice, although I think she's a bit shy*

Expansión

1 Phrases expressing opinions

Personal opinions may also be expressed in any of the following ways:

A mi parecer (*in my opinion*)

A mi parecer no debemos aceptar su oferta	*In my opinion we mustn't accept his offer*
A mi parecer hay que decirle la verdad	*In my opinion, we should tell him the truth*

A mi juicio (*in my opinion*)

A mi juicio, ella no es capaz para este puesto	*In my opinion, she's not capable for this job*

A mi juicio, debemos quejar-
nos a la gerencia

*In my opinion, we should
complain to the manage-
ment*

En mi opinión (*in my opinion*)

En mi opinión, es necesario
vender todo

*In my opinion, it's necessary
to sell everything*

En mi opinión, no podemos
comprar a ese precio

*In my opinion, we can't buy
at that price*

15 Referring to future plans and events

Nota preliminar

Future plans, such as *I am going to buy a house* and *They are going to get married*, and future events, for example *The party will be tomorrow at 8.00* and *The president will arrive on Sunday*, may be expressed in Spanish in more than one way. Constructions like the above have an equivalent in Spanish, although their usage and frequency is not exactly parallel to English. The following grammar below will give you information about when and how to use them.

Have a look at these examples and their English translation before going on to the **Resumen gramatical**.

Asking and answering questions about future plans

Voy a comprar una casa	*I'm going to buy a house*
Van a casarse	*They're going to get married*
¿Cómo viajarás?	*How will you travel?*
Viajaré en coche	*I'll travel by car*

Asking and answering questions about future events

La fiesta será mañana a las 8.00	*The party will be tomorrow at 8.00*
El presidente llegará el domingo	*The president will arrive on Sunday*
¿Dónde será la reunión?	*Where will the meeting be?*
La reunión será aquí	*The meeting will be here*

Resumen gramatical

1 *Ir a* + infinitive

Future plans and intentions are normally expressed with the present tense of **ir (voy, vas, va, vamos, vais, van)** followed by the preposition **a** and an infinitive. This construction is equivalent in English to *to be going to* + infinitive. It is popular in Spanish and it is often used to replace the future tense. Here are some further examples:

¿Qué **vas a** hacer esta noche?	*What are you going to do tonight?*
Voy a salir a cenar	*I'm going out for dinner*
¿Cuándo **vais a** volver?	*When are you going to return?*
Vamos a volver el sábado	*We're going to return on Saturday*
¿Cuánto le **va a** pagar?	*How much is he going to pay you?*
Me **va a** pagar 200 mil pesetas	*He's going to pay me 200 thousand pesetas*

2 Future tense

Uses

The future tense has become less common in the spoken language where it is being gradually replaced by the construction explained earlier. Nowadays its use is restricted more to certain contexts. In formal written language such as that of the Press, for instance, the future tense is very frequent. In spoken language it is often used in sentences expressing promises, commands and a certain degree of uncertainty.

Formation

To form the future tense you use the infinitive followed by the ending, which is the same for the three conjugations. Here are the future forms of three regular verbs representing each of the three conjugations.

estar (*to be*)		**ver** (*to see*)	
estaré	*I will be*	veré	*I will see*
estarás	*you will be* (fam.)	verás	*you will see* (fam.)
estará	*you/he/she will be*	verá	*you/he/she will see*
estaremos	*we will be*	veremos	*we will see*
estaréis	*you will be* (fam.)	veréis	*you will see* (fam.)
estarán	*you/they will be*	verán	*you/they will see*

ir (*to go*)			
iré	*I will go*	iremos	*we will go*
irás	*you will go* (fam.)	iréis	*you will go* (fam.)
irá	*you/he/she will go*	irán	*you/they will go*

Examples:

Press language:
El presidente de Venezuela llegará a Barajas a las 7.30 horas, donde será recibido por el presidente del gobierno español. *The president of Venezuela will arrive in Caracas at 7.30, where he will be received by the president of the Spanish government.*

La nueva fábrica de automóviles que se instalará en Zaragoza iniciará su producción el 30 de junio próximo. *The new car factory which will be installed in Zaragoza will start production on the 30th of June.*

Expressing promises:

Te lo daré mañana	*I'll give it to you tomorrow*
No se lo contaré	*I won't tell him*

Expressing commands:

Os quedaréis aquí	*You'll stay here*
Lo terminarás inmediatamente	*You'll finish it immediately*

Expressing a degree of uncertainty:

Irás a Francia, ¿verdad?	*You'll go to France, won't you?*
Me ayudarás, ¿no?	*You will help me, won't you?*

Irregular future forms

Some verbs have an irregular stem in the future tense but the endings are the same as those of regular verbs. Here is a list of the most important

decir (*to say, tell*)	diré, dirás, dirá, diremos, diréis, dirán
haber (*to have*, auxiliary)	habré, habrás, habrá, habremos, habréis, habrán
hacer (*to do, make*)	haré, harás, hará, haremos, haréis, harán
obtener (*to obtain*)	obtendré, obtendrás, obtendrá, obtendremos, obtendréis, obtendrán
poder (*can, be able to*)	podré, podrás, podrá, podremos, podréis, podrán
poner (*to put*)	pondré, pondrás, pondrá, pondremos, pondréis, pondrán
querer (*to want*)	querré, querrás, querrá, querremos, querréis, querrán

saber (*to know*)	sabré, sabrás, sabrá,
	sabremos, sabréis, sabrán
salir (*to go out*)	saldré, saldrás, saldrá,
	saldremos, saldréis, saldrán
tener (*to have*)	tendré, tendrás, tendrá,
	tendremos, tendréis, tendrán
venir (*to come*)	vendré, vendrás, vendrá,
	vendremos, vendréis, vendrán

Nota: For a list of the most common irregular verbs see pages 221–226 of **Apuntes gramaticales**.

Examples:

¿Qué harás mañana?	*What will you do tomorrow?*
Saldré con Ana	*I'll go out with Ana*
Tendrás que decírmelo	*You'll have to tell me*
No te lo diré	*I won't tell you*
Podrá Vd. venir el lunes,	*You'll be able to come on*
¿verdad?	*Monday, won't you?*
Creo que no podré	*I don't think I'll be able to*

En contexto

1 *Victor and Mercedes talk about their summer holiday.*

Víctor	¿Qué vais a hacer tú y Pablo este verano?
Mercedes	Vamos a ir a Buenos Aires a visitar a unos parientes.
Víctor	¿Vais con los chicos?
Mercedes	No, ellos van a quedarse con los abuelos en Madrid.
Víctor	¿Cuánto tiempo vais a estar allí?
Mercedes	Un mes solamente. Vamos a volver a finales de agosto. ¿Y tú qué planes tienes? ¿Irás otra vez a San Antonio?
Víctor	No, esta vez iré a casa de unos amigos en Ibiza.
Mercedes	Ibiza te va a gustar mucho. Es un lugar precioso. ¿Vas a quedarte mucho tiempo?

Victor	Un par de semanas. Tendré que volver antes del quince pues viene Marta a pasar unos días conmigo . . .

unos parientes	*some relatives*
a finales de	*at the end of*
otra vez	*again*
esta vez	*this time*
un par de semanas	*a couple of weeks*
a pasar unos días	*to spend some days*

2 *Read this paragraph from the Press.*

El 1 de abril próximo llegará a nuestro país en visita oficial el ministro de asuntos exteriores británico Sir John Perkins, quien se entrevistará con el jefe del gobierno español. El ministro permanecerá en Madrid por espacio de tres días y en las conversaciones que sostendrá con las autoridades de gobierno se tratará el tema de Gibraltar . . .

el ministro de asuntos exteriores	*minister of foreign affairs*
se entrevistará	*he will meet/will have a meeting*
permanecerá	*he will remain*
por espacio de	*for, during*
las conversaciones	*talks*
que sostendrá	*that he will hold*
las autoridades	*authorities*
se tratará	*they will deal with*
el tema	*subject*

Explicaciones

Ellos van a quedarse en casa	*They are going to stay at home*

An alternative position for the reflexive pronoun in this sentence would be before the finite verb: **ellos se van a quedar en casa**. Likewise:

¿vas a quedarte mucho tiempo? or ¿te vas a quedar mucho tiempo? (*are you going to stay long?*).

Expansión

1   Present tense with future meaning

As in English, Spanish also uses the present tense to refer to the future, particularly to the immediate future and with verbs which indicate movement (e.g., **ir**, *to go*; **salir**, *to go out*; **venir**, *to come*), but also with the verb **hacer** (*to do*). Time phrases such as **mañana** (*tomorrow*), **pasado mañana** (*the day after tomorrow*) **la semana que viene** (*next week*), **el mes que viene** (*next month*), **la semana próxima** (*next week*), **el mes próximo** (*next month*), etc., will make it clear that the time reference is the future and not the present. Here are some examples:

¿Qué haces **mañana**? — What are you doing tomorrow?

Voy a la piscina — I'm going to the swimming pool

Salimos **pasado mañana** — We leave the day after tomorrow

Él llega la **semana que viene** — He is arriving next week

2   *Pensar* to refer to plans and intentions

Pensar (*to think, to be thinking of*) is often used to refer to future plans and intentions in sentences like these:

¿Qué **piensas** hacer este verano? — What are you thinking of doing this summer?

Pienso ir a Nueva York — I'm thinking of going to New York

¿Cuándo **piensas** volver? — When are you thinking of coming back?

Pensamos casarnos   *We're thinking of getting married*

3 The future of probability

The future tense is often used to express probability or conjecture in sentences like these:

¿Qué hora **será**?   *I wonder what time it is?/ what time can it be?*

Serán las dos   *It must be 2.00 o'clock*
¿Dónde **estará** María?   *I wonder where Maria is/ where can Maria be?*

16 Making requests and offers

Objetivos

In this Unit you will learn how to:

Make requests • Reply to a request • Make offers
• Reply to offers

Contenido gramatical

Present tense in requests and offers • 'poder' in requests
and offers • 'querer' in requests and offers • 'podría' in
requests

Nota preliminar

When we make requests and offers in English we can do this in a
number of ways. Consider for instance the following sentences: *Will
you help me, please?*, *Can you show me the way?*, *Shall I carry your
suitcase?*, *Can I make you some coffee?* and *Do you want some biscuits?*
Spanish too, has several ways of expressing these ideas. The notes
below will teach you how to construct sentences of this type using
some of the grammar you learned in previous Units.

You will also learn how to reply to a request or an offer. Words and
phrases such as *certainly*, *yes please*, *that's very kind of you*, etc., all
have an equivalent in Spanish.

Have a look at these examples and their English translation before
going on to the **Resumen gramatical**.

Making requests

Me ayuda, por favor	*Will you help me, please?*
¿Puede indicarme el camino, por favor?	*Can you show me the way, please?*

Replying to a request

Por supuesto	*Certainly/of course*
Cómo no	*Certainly*

Making offers

¿Le llevo la maleta?	*Shall I carry your suitcase?*
¿Te preparo un café?	*Can I make you some coffee?*
¿Quieres galletas?	*Do you want some biscuits?*

Replying to offers

Sí, por favor	*Yes, please*
Es Vd. muy amable	*That's very kind of you*

Resumen gramatical

1 Present tense in requests and offers

Requests

A frequent way of making requests is by using the present tense preceded by an object pronoun, for example

Me despierta a las 7.00, por favor	*Will you wake me at 7.00 please?*

Nos llama a las 8.00, por favor	*Will you call us at 8.00, please?*
Me pasa la sal	*Will you pass the salt?*
Nos llama un taxi	*Will you call a taxi for us?*
Le dice a Gloria que estoy aquí, por favor	*Will you tell Gloria I'm here, please?*

Offers

The same construction – present tense preceded by an object pronoun – may be used in making offers. Here are some examples:

¿Le doy un poco más?	*Shall I give you some more?*
¿Les reservo una habitación?	*Shall I book a room for you?*
¿Te ayudo?	*Shall I help you?*
¿Os llamo a las 6.00?	*Shall I call you at 6.00?*
¿Os llevo a la estación?	*Shall I take you to the station?*

Replies to the above will vary depending on the degree of formality. Here are some of the most common:

Sí, por favor	*Yes, please*
Es Vd. muy amable	*That's very kind of you*
De acuerdo	*All right*
Vale	*OK*
Bueno	*All right*

2   *Poder* in requests and offers

Requests

Poder (*can, be able to*) is used in requests in sentences like these:

¿**Puede** llamar al Sr. Martínez, por favor?	*Can you call señor Martínez, please?*

¿**Pueden** darnos otra mesa, por favor?	*Can you give us another table, please?*
¿**Puede** Vd. cambiarme este dinero?	*Can you change this money for me?*
¿**Puede** Vd. ayudarnos?	*Can you help us?*

Notice that the object pronoun may also be placed before the finite verb, **poder**:

| ¿**Nos** pueden dar otra mesa, por favor? | *Can you give us another table, please?* |
| ¿**Me** puede Vd. cambiar este dinero? | *Can you change this money for me?* |

Offers

Poder may also be used in making offers, as in

¿**Puedo** llevarla a su hotel?	*May I take you to your hotel?*
¿**Puedo** hacer algo por Vd.?	*Can I do something for you?*
¿**Podemos** ayudarle?	*Can we help you?*

En contexto

1 *At the hotel reception.*

Viajera	Buenas noches. Me marcho mañana a las 8.00. ¿Puede Vd. llamarme a las 7.00 por favor?
Recepcionista	Sí, cómo no. ¿Le envío el desayuno a la habitación?
Viajera	Sí, por favor. Y me da la cuenta también. Quiero pagarla ahora mismo.
Recepcionista	De acuerdo, señora.
Viajera	Ah, necesito un taxi para mañana. ¿Puede Vd. llamarme uno para las 8.00 si es tan amable?

Recepcionista	Por supuesto. Es para ir al aeropuerto, ¿verdad?
Viajera	Sí, tengo que estar allí a las 8.45.
Recepcionista	Muy bien, señora. Yo mismo le llamaré uno. No se preocupe Vd.
Viajera	Muchas gracias.

¿le envío el desayuno . . . ?	*shall I send your breakfast . . . ?*
me da la cuenta	*will you give me the bill?*
ahora mismo	*right now*
si es tan amable	*if you are kind enough*
yo mismo	*I myself*
no se preocupe	*don't worry*

2 *A request note.*

Raúl,

¿Puedes pasar por mi despacho antes de irte a casa?
Necesito hablar urgentemente contigo. Es importante.

Alfonso

pasar por	*to drop in*
urgentemente	*urgently*

Explicaciones

¿Puede Vd. llamarme a las 7.00, por favor?	*Can you call me at 7.00, please?*

This construction is slightly more formal and polite than the alternative **me llama Vd. a las 7.00, por favor**.

The latter, however, seems to be more frequent overall, probably due to its simplicity. Notice the sentence:

Y me da la cuenta también	*Will you give me the bill too*

Expansión

1 *Querer* used in requests

Querer (*to want*) is used in requests in sentences like these:

¿**Quiere** esperar un momento, por favor?	*Would you wait a moment, please?*
¿**Quiere** dejarlo aquí, por favor?	*Would you leave it here, please?*
¿**Quiere** repetir si es tan amable?	*Would you be kind enough to repeat that?*

2 *Querer* in offers

Querer may also be used in offers:

¿**Quieres** un poco más de café?	*Do you want some more coffee?*
¿**Quieres** una copa?	*Do you want a drink?*
¿**Quiere** Vd. que le llame?	*Do you want me to call you?*
¿**Quieren** Vds. que les llevemos al aeropuerto?	*Do you want us to take you to the airport?*

The last two examples are sentences with a main clause ¿**quiere Vd.**?, ¿**quieren Vds.**? followed by a subordinate clause containing a subjunctive: **que le llame, que les llevemos al aeropuerto**. For an explanation of the subjunctive see Unit 21.

3 *Podría* used in requests

Podría, a form which corresponds to the 1st and 3rd person singular of the conditional tense (see Unit 22), is often used in making more polite and formal requests.

¿**Podría** traerme un vaso de agua?	*Would you bring me a glass of water?*
¿**Podría** Vd. hablar más despacio?	*Would you speak more slowly?*

To address more than one person we use **podrían**:

¿**Podrían** Vds. pagar la cuenta ahora?	*Would you pay the bill now?*
¿**Podrían** Vds. dejar la habitación antes de las 12.00?	*Would you leave your room before 12.00?*

17 Referring to the recent past

Nota preliminar

Past events which bear relationship with the present, for example *She's sad because she's had some bad news* or *Why have you done this?*, are normally expressed in English through the perfect tense. The perfect tense is also used to relate events which have taken place over a period of time which includes the present, as in *She hasn't been here today* or *I've seen this film twice this week*. Spanish also uses the perfect tense to express the same ideas (see examples below). Usage differs, however, when we relate recent events such as *I met Peter a while ago*, or *Did you hear that noise?* To relate events like these English normally uses the simple past while Peninsular Spanish prefers the perfect tense.

The grammar notes below will give you ample information on how to form and use the Spanish perfect tense. Examples are also given of **acabar de** + infinitive, another construction used when talking about the recent past, which has an equivalent in English in *to have just* + past participle, e.g. *She has just gone out*.

Have a look at these examples and their English translation before going on to the **Resumen gramatical**.

Referring to past events which bear relation to the present

¿Qué le ha pasado a Dolores?	*What has happened to Dolores?*
Dolores está triste porque ha recibido una mala noticia	*Dolores is sad because she's had some bad news*
¿Por qué has hecho esto?	*Why have you done this?*

Referring to events which have taken place over a period of time which includes the present

Ella no ha estado aquí hoy	*She hasn't been here today*
He visto esta película dos veces esta semana	*I've seen this film twice this week*

Referring to the recent past

Me he encontrado con Peter hace un rato	*I met Peter a while ago*
¿Has oído ese ruido?	*Did you hear that noise?*

Resumen gramatical

1 Perfect tense

Usage

As explained in the **Nota preliminar,** the Spanish perfect tense is used to relate past events which bear relationship with the present, to relate events which have taken place over a period of time which includes the present and to relate recent events.

Formation

To form the perfect tense we use the present tense of **haber** (*to have*) followed by a past participle which is invariable. Remember that the past participle of **-ar** verbs ends in **-ado** while **-er** and **-ir** verbs form the past participle by adding **-ido** to the stem. For irregular past participles see pages 99–100

estudiar (*to study*)	
he estudiado	*I have studied*
has estudiado	*you have studied* (fam.)
ha estudiado	*you have studied*
	he/she has studied
hemos estudiado	*we have studied*
habéis estudiado	*you have studied* (fam.)
han estudiado	*you/they have studied*

comer (*to eat*)	
he comido	*I have eaten*
has comido	*you have eaten* (fam.)
ha comido	*you have eaten*
	he/she has eaten
hemos comido	*we have eaten*
habéis comido	*you have eaten* (fam.)
han comido	*you/they have eaten*

salir (*to go out*)	
he salido	*I have gone out*
has salido	*you have gone out* (fam.)
ha salido	*you have gone out*
hemos salido	*we have gone out*
habéis salido	*you have gone out* (fam.)
han salido	*you/they have gone out*

Examples:

He estudiado español toda la tarde	*I have studied Spanish the whole afternoon*
¿Por qué no **has estudiado**?	*Why haven't you studied?*
¿**Has comido** suficiente?	*Have you eaten enough?*
He comido bastante	*I've eaten enough*
Carmen **ha salido** hace un rato	*Carmen went out a while ago*
No **he salido** en toda la semana	*I haven't been out this week*

Here are some examples with irregular past participles:

¿**Has visto** a Mario?	*Have you seen Mario?*
Le **he visto** dos veces esta semana	*I've seen him twice this week*
¿Qué **has hecho** hoy?	*What have you done today?*
No **he hecho** nada	*I haven't done anything*
¿Qué **ha dicho** Pedro?	*What has Pedro said?*
No sé lo que **ha dicho**	*I don't know what he's said*
Luis **ha vuelto** de Londres	*Luis has come back from London*

2 *Acabar de* + infinitive

To express what we have just done we use the verb **acabar** (literally, *to finish*) in the present tense followed by the preposition **de** and an infinitive.

Ella **acaba de** salir	*She has just gone out*
Acabo de llegar	*I've just arrived*
Acabamos de verle	*We've just seen him*
Acaban de marcharse	*They've just left*

En contexto

1   *Isabel is looking for her friend Enrique.*

Isabel   Buenas tardes. ¿Está Enrique?

Señora   Lo siento, pero Enrique no está. Acaba de salir. Ha ido a casa de José.

Isabel   Por favor, ¿puede Vd. decirle que le he venido a buscar para ir a la piscina? Le esperaré allí.

Señora   Sí, cómo no. Se lo diré.

Isabel   Hasta luego, gracias.

Señora   De nada, hasta luego.

| **le he venido a buscar** | *I've come for him* |
| **le esperaré allí** | *I'll wait for him there* |

2   *What have you done today?*

Él   ¿Qué has hecho hoy?

Ella   Esta mañana he estado en la biblioteca un rato y he terminado de escribir un artículo para la clase de mañana. Luego he ido a la peluquería. Acabo de regresar. ¿Y tú qué has hecho?

Él   Hoy me he levantado muy tarde y me he quedado en casa leyendo. ¿Has comido ya?

Ella   No, todavía no. No he tenido tiempo de preparar nada.

Él   Entonces, ¿qué te parece si vamos a comer algo? Podemos ir al bar de Pepe.

Ella   De acuerdo, vamos.

la biblioteca	*library*
un artículo	*article*
la peluquería	*hairdresser's*
¿has comido ya?	*have you eaten already?*
todavía no	*not yet*

Explicaciones

Me he levantado tarde	*I got up late*
Me he quedado en casa	*I stayed at home*

Notice the position of the pronouns in these two sentences. Pronouns always precede the construction with the perfect tense.

Expansion

1 Spanish American usage

The perfect tense is much less frequent in Spanish America than in Peninsular Spanish. To refer to recent events Latin Americans prefer to use the simple past, for example **terminé** (*I finished*) for **he terminado** (*I have finished*), **hoy me levanté tarde** (*today I got up late*) for **hoy me he levantado tarde** (*today I've got up late*). The same holds true when relating events which are somehow linked to the present, as in **¿viste esta película?** (*did you see this film?*) instead of **¿has visto esta película?** (*have you seen this film?*), **¿leíste este libro?** (*did you read this book?*) instead of **¿has leído este libro?** (*have you read this book?*). However, bear in mind that this is a matter of frequency of use rather than total exclusion of the perfect tense. Both tenses are actually used and will be understood by Spanish speakers.

Nota: For the uses and formation of the simple past tense refer to Unit 18).

18 Referring to past events

Objetivos

In this Unit you will learn how to:

Refer to events which are past and complete • Refer to events which lasted over a definite period of time and ended in the past

Contenido gramatical

Preterite tense • Adverbs of time associated with the preterite • 'Hace' in time phrases • Historic present

Nota preliminar

To refer to events which happened and were completed in the past, as in *They went to Chile last year* or *He died two years ago*, Spanish uses the preterite tense or simple past.

Events wich lasted over a definite period of time and ended in the past, for instance *She lived in England for seven years* or *We worked together for a month*, are also expressed in Spanish through the preterite. Certain time phrases such as **el año pasado** (*last year*), **ayer** (*yesterday*), **el lunes pasado** (*last Monday*), etc., are normally associated with this tense.

In the grammar notes below you will find information about how to form and actually use the preterite tense. Have a look at these

examples and their English translation before going on to the
Resumen gramatical.

Referring to events which are past and complete

El año pasado fueron a Chile	*They went to Chile last year*
Murió hace dos años	*He died two years ago*
¿Cuándo llegaste?	*When did you arrive?*
Llegué el lunes pasado	*I arrived last Monday*
¿Dónde nació Vd.?	*Where were you born?*
Nací en México	*I was born in Mexico*

Referring to events which lasted over a definite period of time and ended in the past

Ella vivió en Inglaterra durante siete años	*She lived in England for seven years*
Trabajamos juntas durante un mes	*We worked together for a month*
¿Cuánto tiempo estudiaste allí?	*How long did you study there?*
Estudié allí durante cuatro meses	*I studied there for four months*

Resumen gramatical

1   Preterite tense

Usage

As explained in the **Nota preliminar**, the preterite is normally used to
refer to events which are past and complete and to events which lasted
over a definite period of time and ended in the past.

Formation

There are two sets of endings for this tense, one for **-ar** verbs and another one for verbs in **-er** and **-ir**.

viajar (*to travel*)	
viajé	*I travelled*
viajaste	*you travelled* (fam.)
viajó	*you/he/she travelled*
viajamos	*we travelled*
viajasteis	*you travelled* (fam.)
viajaron	*you/they travelled*

Note that the 1st person plural, **viajamos**, is the same as for the present tense.

responder (*to answer*)	
respondí	*I answered*
respondiste	*you answered* (fam.)
respondió	*you/he/she answered*
respondimos	*we answered*
respondisteis	*you answered* (fam.)
respondieron	*you/they answered*

recibir (*to receive*)	
recibí	*I received*
recibiste	*you received* (fam.)
recibió	*you/he/she received*
recibimos	*we received*
recibisteis	*you received* (fam.)
recibieron	*you/they received*

Note that the 1st person plural, **recibimos**, is the same as for the present tense.

Examples:

El año pasado **viajé** a Perú	*Last year I travelled to Peru*
El **viajó** por más de una semana.	*He travelled for more than a week*
Ayer **respondí** a la carta de Esteban	*I answered Esteban's letter yesterday*
Carlos no **respondió** a mi carta	*Carlos didn't answer my letter*
¿Cuándo **recibiste** el paquete?	*When did you receive the parcel?*
Lo **recibí** el martes pasado.	*I received it last Tuesday*

Irregular preterite forms

Some verbs have an irregular preterite. Here is a list of the most important.

andar (*to walk*)	anduve, anduviste, anduvo, anduvimos, anduvisteis, anduvieron
estar (*to be*)	estuve, estuviste, estuvo, estuvimos, estuvisteis, estuvieron,
haber (*to have*, aux.)	hube, hubiste, hubo, hubimos, hubisteis, hubieron
obtener (*to get*)	obtuve, obtuviste, obtuvo, obtuvimos, obtuvisteis, obtuvieron
tener (*to have*)	tuve, tuviste, tuvo, tuvimos, tuvisteis, tuvieron
saber (*to know*)	supe, supiste, supo, supimos, supisteis, supieron
poner (*to put*)	puse, pusiste, puso, pusimos, pusisteis, pusieron
suponer (*to suppose*)	supuse, supusiste, supuso, supusimos, supusisteis, supusieron
dar (*to give*)	di, diste, dio, dimos, disteis, dieron
decir (*to say*)	dije, dijiste, dijo, dijimos, dijisteis, dijeron
hacer (*to do, make*)	hice, hiciste, hizo, hicimos, hicisteis, hicieron

querer *(to want)*	quise, quisiste, quiso, quisimos, quisisteis, quisieron
venir *(to come)*	vine, viniste, vino, vinimos, vinisteis, vinieron
traer *(to bring)*	traje, trajiste, trajo, trajimos, trajisteis, trajeron
ir *(to go)*	fui, fuiste, fue, fuimos, fuisteis, fueron
ser *(to be)*	fui, fuiste, fue, fuimos, fuisteis, fueron

Nota: For a list of the most common irregular verbs see pages 221–226 of **Apuntes gramaticales**.

Examples:

¿Qué **hiciste** ayer?	*What did you do yesterday?*
Fui a casa de Manolo	*I went to Manolo's house*
¿Dónde **estuvisteis** este verano?	*Where were you this summer?*
Estuvimos en San Francisco	*We were in San Francisco*
¿Qué le **diste** a Roberto para su cumpleaños?	*What did you give Roberto for his birthday?*
Le **di** una corbata	*I gave him a tie*

Spelling changes in the preterite tense

Some verbs need a change in the spelling in the 1st person singular to enable the final consonant of the stem to keep the same sound as in the infinitive. Some of these verbs are:

llegar	*to arrive*	llegué	*I arrived*
pagar	*to pay*	pagué	*I paid*
sacar	*to get*, e.g. tickets	saqué	*I got*
tocar	*to play an instrument*	toqué	*I played*

A spelling change may also occur because of an accent in the infinitive or because there would otherwise be more than two vowels together:

caer (*to fall*)	caí, caíste, cayó, caímos, caísteis, cayeron
leer (*to read*)	leí, leíste, leyó, leímos, leísteis, leyeron
oír (*to hear*)	oí, oíste, oyó, oímos, oísteis, oyeron

Examples:

Llegué hace dos semanas	*I arrived two weeks ago*
Pagué la cuenta anoche	*I paid the bill last night*
Saqué dos entradas para el cine	*I got two tickets for the cinema*
Ella no **leyó** la carta	*She didn't read the letter*

2   Adverbs of time and time phrases normally associated with the preterite tense

The following adverbs of time and time phrases often occur in sentences with a verb in the preterite tense:

ayer	*yesterday*
anteayer	*the day before yesterday*
anoche	*last night*
el lunes/martes pasado	*last Monday/Tuesday*
la semana pasada	*last week*
el mes/el año pasado	*last month/year*
en 1975/en 1980	*in 1975/in 1980*
hace dos meses/tres años	*two months/three years ago*

Nota: some of these time phrases may also occur with other tenses, for example the imperfect tense (see Unit 19).

3 *Hace* in time phrases

Note the two different translations of **hace** in the sentences below.

(*a*) With a verb in the present tense (**hace** = *for*)

Vive aquí desde **hace** dos años	He's been living here for two years
Hace seis meses que estoy en Madrid	I've been in Madrid for six months

(*b*) With a verb in the preterite tense (**hace** = *ago*)

Vivió aquí **hace** dos años	He lived here two years ago
Hace seis meses estuve en Madrid	I was in Madrid six months ago
¿Cuánto tiempo **hace** que llegaste?	How long ago did you arrive?
¿Cuántos años **hace** que murió?	How many years ago did he die?

Nota: For the use of **hace** with a present tense verb see **Expansión** in Unit 8.

En contexto

1 *What did you do on your holiday?*

Marisol	¿Qué hiciste en tus vacaciones?
Fernando	Estuve unos días en Inglaterra en casa de unos amigos.
Marisol	¿Fuiste solo?
Fernando	No, fui con Angela.
Marisol	¿Y qué os pareció Londres?

Fernando   Nos gustó muchísimo. Lo pasamos estupendamente. ¿Y tú has estado alguna vez en Inglaterra?

Marisol   Sí, estuve allí hace cuatro años. Hice un curso de inglés en Brighton y viví un mes con una familia inglesa. Lo pasé muy bien. Pienso volver el año que viene.

Fernando   Si vas te daré el teléfono de mis amigos. Son muy simpáticos y estoy seguro que te gustarán.

¿qué os pareció Londres?	*what did you think of London?*
lo pasamos estupendamente	*we had a very good time*
alguna vez	*ever*
un curso de inglés	*an English course*
lo pasé muy bien	*I had a good time*
estoy seguro	*I'm sure*

2   *The manager has been away from the office for a few days. On his return he talks to his secretary.*

Gerente   ¿Hay algún recado para mí?

Secretaria   Sí, el lunes llamó el señor Solís para pedir una cita con usted. Vendrá mañana a las 10.00. También hubo una llamada del señor Francisco Riquelme de México. Dice que llegará a Madrid el viernes a las 2.00 de la tarde.

Gerente   ¿Han traído el nuevo ordenador?

Secretaria   Sí, lo trajeron ayer. Lo dejaron en su despacho. Aquí está la factura.

¿hay algún recado?	*is there any message?*
pedir una cita	*to ask for an appointment*
hubo una llamada	*there was a call*
el ordenador	*computer*
la factura	*invoice*

Explicaciones

Observe the contrast between the perfect tense and the preterite tense in these two sentences:

¿Y tú has estado alguna vez   *and have you ever been to*
  en Inglaterra?   *England?*
Estuve allí hace cuatro años   *I was there four years ago*

The two tenses are not interchangeable in these sentences. Words like **alguna vez** (*ever*), **nunca** (*never*) require the use of the perfect tense because they somehow establish a relationship with the present: **alguna vez** (*ever*) is equivalent in meaning to **hasta ahora** (*so far*). In the second sentence, the preterite tense is obligatory because it refers to an event which is past and complete.

Expansión

1   Historic present

The present tense is frequently used in narrative contexts (e.g. literature, history) with a past meaning in order to lend more force to the actions or events being described. It is also present in colloquial language.

Written language

En noviembre de 1975 muere el general Francisco Franco y el príncipe Juan Carlos pasa a ocupar el trono de España. El país empieza a vivir una serie de cambios de orden político y social . . .

General Francisco Franco died in November 1975 and Prince Juan Carlos occupied the Spanish throne. The country began to undergo a series of political and social changes . . .

Spoken language

> Esta mañana en el metro he visto a Antonia. Sabes, se acerca a mí
> y me dice que siente mucho lo ocurrido . . .
> *This morning, in the underground, I saw Antonia. You know, she
> came up to me and told me that she was very sorry about what
> happened . . .*

In both of the above examples, depending on the context, the present
tense could be used in the English translation.

19 Describing the past

Objetivos

In this Unit you will learn how to:

Describe things, places and people with reference to the past • Describe actions which were taking place when something else happened • Describe states or actions which were habitual in the past • Describe states or actions which occurred before some past event

Contenido gramatical

Imperfect tense • Imperfect continuous • Pluperfect tense • 'Soler' + infinitive for past reference • 'Acostumbrar a' + infinitive for past reference

Nota preliminar

To describe things, places and people with reference to the past, as in *It was a large suitcase*, *It was a nice town* and *She had long hair*, we normally use the imperfect tense. We also use the imperfect tense to describe actions which were taking place when something else happened, for example *She was reading when he gave her the news* or *I was working when the telephone rang*. The same tense is used to describe states or actions which were habitual in the past, for instance *We used to get up at 7.00 every day* and *They used to visit us every summer*. In the grammar notes below you will find information about how to form and use the imperfect tense.

You will also learn to describe states or actions which occurred before some past event, as in *She had already gone out when you called.* For this you will need another tense called the pluperfect.

Finally, you will learn some idiomatic constructions used in Spanish to refer to states or actions which were habitual in the past.

Have a look at these examples and their English translation before going on to the **Resumen gramatical**.

Describing things, places and people with reference to the past

Era una maleta grande	*It was a large suitcase*
Era una ciudad bonita	*It was a nice town*
Tenía el pelo largo	*She had long hair*

Describing actions which were taking place when something else happened

	Ella leía cuando él le dio la noticia	*She was reading when he gave her the news*
or,		
	Ella estaba leyendo cuando él le dio la noticia	*She was reading when he gave her the news*
	Yo trabajaba cuando sonó el teléfono	*I was working when the telephone rang*
or,		
	Yo estaba trabajando cuando sonó el teléfono	*I was working when the telephone rang*

Describing states or actions which were habitual in the past

Nos levantábamos a las 7.00 todos los días	*We used to get up at 7.00 everyday*
Nos visitaban todos los veranos	*They used to visit us every summer*

Describing states or actions which occurred before some past event

Ella ya había salido cuando
la llamaste

*She had already gone out
when you called*

Yo había terminado de
cenar cuando ellos
llegaron

*I had finished dinner when
they arrived*

Resumen gramatical

1   Imperfect tense

Uses

In general terms, the imperfect tense is used for actions which were taking place in the past and whose beginning or end are not specified. Unlike the preterite, which commonly indicates completed past events, the imperfect denotes actions which were incomplete. Consider these two sentences:

En aquel tiempo yo
trabajaba en Barcelona

*At that time I used to work
in Barcelona*

Entre enero y junio de ese
año trabajé en Barcelona

*Between January and June of
that year I worked in
Barcelona*

In the first example, the beginning and end of the action are not specified. In the second sentence we are referring to a completed past event.

More specifically, and as stated in the **Nota preliminar**, the imperfect tense is used to describe things, places and people with reference to the past, to describe actions which were taking place when something else happened (the second action will normally be expressed in the preterite) and to describe states or actions which were habitual in the past. Study now the formation of the imperfect tense and then consider again the sentences under **Nota preliminar** and the further examples below.

Formation

There are two sets of endings for the imperfect tense, one for **-ar** verbs and another one for verbs ending in **-er** and **-ir**.

	trabajar (*to work*)
trabajaba	*I worked/used to work*
trabajabas	*you worked/used to work* (fam.)
trabajaba	*you/he/she worked/used to work*
trabajábamos	*we worked/used to work*
trabajabais	*you worked/used to work* (fam.)
trabajaban	*you/they worked/used to work*

Note that the 1st and 3rd person singular share the same endings.

	tener (*to have*)
tenía	*I had/used to have*
tenías	*you had/used to have* (fam.)
tenía	*you/he/she/it had/used to have*
teníamos	*we had/used to have*
teníais	*you had/used to have* (fam.)
tenían	*you/they had/used to have*

	vivir (*to live*)
vivía	*I lived/used to live*
vivías	*you lived/used to live* (fam.)
vivía	*you/he/she lived/used to live*
vivíamos	*we lived/used to live*
vivíais	*you lived/used to live* (fam.)
vivían	*you/they lived/used to live*

Note that the 1st and 3rd person singular share the same endings.

Examples:

¿Dónde **trabajabas** antes?	*Where did you work/were you working before?*
Trabajaba en una fábrica	*I worked/was working/used to work in a factory*
¿Qué coche **tenía** Vd. antes?	*What car did you have before?*
Tenía un Seat 127	*I had a Seat 127*
¿Dónde **vivíais** antes de llegar aquí?	*Where did you live before arriving here?*
Vivíamos en Toledo	*We lived/used to live in Toledo*

Irregular imperfect forms

There are only three irregular verbs in the imperfect tense:

ir (*to go*), **ser** (*to be*) and **ver** (*to see*).

ir	ser	ver
iba	era	veía
ibas (fam.)	eras (fam.)	veías (fam.)
iba	era	veía
íbamos	éramos	veíamos
ibais (fam.)	erais (fam.)	veíais
iban	eran	veían

Nota. For a list of the most common irregular verbs in all tenses see pages 222–227 of **Apuntes gramaticales**.

Examples:

Yo **iba** al colegio cuando ocurrió el accidente.	*I was going to school when the accident happened*
Javier **iba** a Granada todos los años.	*Javier used to go to Granada every year*

¿Cómo **era** Patricia?	*What was Patricia like?*
Patricia **era** alta, delgada y tenía los ojos verdes.	*Patricia was tall, slim and she had green eyes*
¿Cómo **era** la casa donde vivías?	*What was the house where you lived like?*
Era una casa grande y moderna y tenía un gran jardín	*It was a big modern house and it had a large garden*
Francisca y yo nos **veíamos** casi todos los días	*Francisca and I used to see each other almost everyday*
Ellos siempre **veían** la televisión después de cenar	*They always watched television after having dinner*

2   Imperfect continuous

Usage

To make it clear we are referring to an action which was in process when something else happened, for example *I was eating when he called me*, we can use the imperfect continuous as an alternative to the imperfect tense.

Formation

The imperfect continuous is formed with the imperfect form of **estar** followed by a gerund (for the present continuous, see Unit 8). Here are some examples:

Ella **estaba preparando** el almuerzo cuando él entró	*She was preparing lunch when he came in*
Nosotros **estábamos durmiendo** cuando ocurrió el robo	*We were sleeping when the theft took place*
¿Qué **estabas haciendo** allí?	*What were you doing there?*
Estaba hablando con Marta	*I was talking to Marta*

¿A quién **estabas llamando**?	*Who were you calling?*
Estaba llamando a Alberto	*I was calling Alberto*

3 Pluperfect tense

Usage

The Spanish pluperfect tense is equivalent to the English pluperfect
and it is normally used to describe states or actions which occurred
before some past event, as in *Her mother had died when John was born.*

Formation

The pluperfect tense is formed with the imperfect form of **haber (había,
habías, había, habíamos, habíais, habían)** followed by a past participle
which is invariable (for the formation of past participles see Unit 11).
Examples:

La reunión ya **había** empezado cuando nosotros entramos.	*The meeting had already started when we went in*
La fiesta ya **había** terminado cuando empezó a llover.	*The party had already finished when it started to rain*
No aceptamos su invitación pues ya **habíamos** visto la película.	*We didn't accept their invitation because we had already seen the film*

En contexto

1 *Remembering the past.*

Ignacio	¿Cuánto tiempo hace que vives aquí?
Eliana	Hace dos años solamente.
Ignacio	¿Y dónde vivías antes?

Eliana	Vivía en Nueva York.
Ignacio	¡En Nueva York! ¿Y qué hacías allí?
Eliana	Trabajaba en un colegio como profesora de español, y al mismo tiempo estudiaba inglés en la universidad. Con lo que ganaba como profesora pagaba mis estudios y el alquiler de un apartamento.
Ignacio	¿Vivías sola?
Eliana	No, compartía el apartamento con dos colegas. Uno era español y el otro colombiano.
Ignacio	¿Hablabas ya inglés cuando llegaste allí.
Eliana	Lo hablaba bastante mal y entendía muy poco, pero conseguí aprender bastante.

al mismo tiempo	*at the same time*
con lo que ganaba	*with what I earned*
el alquiler	*rent*
compartía	*I was sharing*
un/una colega	*colleague*
conseguí aprender	*I managed to learn*

2 *Read this extract from a short story.*

Eran ya las 9.00 de la noche cuando Lucía llegó a la casa de la señora Velarde. Hacía frío y la lluvia empezaba a caer. Lucía llamó a la puerta tres veces pero nadie respondió. La señora Rosario Velarde era una mujer mayor, tenía unos ochenta años, y vivía sola con su perro Damián. Lucía llamó otra vez, pero nadie respondió. Dentro de la casa había luz y por la ventana se veía la pequeña sala . . .

la lluvia empezaba a caer	*the rain was starting to fall*
llamó a la puerta	*she knocked at the door*
una mujer mayor	*an old woman*
tenía unos ochenta años	*she was about eighty years old*
había luz	*there was a light*
por la ventana	*through the window*
la sala	*sitting room*

Explicaciones

Notice the use of the imperfect and preterite tenses in the second text:

hacía frío	*it was cold*
la lluvia empezaba a caer	*the rain was starting to fall*
Lucía llamó a la puerta	*Lucia knocked at the door*
nadie respondió	*no one answered*

Here, the imperfect tense is descriptive while the preterite serves to indicate a series of completed past events.

Expansión

1 *Soler* + infinitive for past reference

In Unit 9 (**Expansión**, page 91) we studied the use of **soler** in the present tense followed by an infinitive to denote an action that occurs regularly (e.g. **suelo levantarme tarde**, *I usually get up late*). The same construction may be used in the imperfect tense to refer to an action which was habitual in the past.

¿Qué **solías** hacer?	*What did you usually do?*
Solía leer mucho	*I used to read a lot*
Solíamos quedarnos en casa	*We used to stay at home*

2 *Acostumbrar a* + infinitive for past reference

Acostumbrar a + infinitive functions in the same way as **soler** + infinitive. It may be used in the present tense (see Unit 9, page 91) to refer to events which occur regularly (e.g. **acostumbro a estudiar por la noche**, *I usually study at night*), or it may be used in the imperfect to denote events which were habitual in the past.

Él **acostumbraba a** pasar largas horas en nuestra casa	*He used to spend long hours at our home*
Acostumbrábamos a vernos una vez por semana	*We used to see each other once a week*
Ellos **acostumbraban a** dar largos paseos al atardecer	*They used to go for long walks in the evening*

20 Giving directions and instructions

Objetivos

In this Unit you will learn how to:

Ask and give directions • Give commands and instructions

Contenido gramatical

Imperative • Present tense used in directions • Infinitive used in directions

---

Nota preliminar

When we give directions in English, we can do so in a number of ways. Consider, for instance, the following sentences: *You can turn right at the corner, You have to cross the road, Continue along this road* and *Turn left here*, etc. Spanish expresses the same ideas in approximately similar ways, although some forms are more frequent than others. The imperative, as seen in the last two examples above – *continue along this road, turn left* – is perhaps one of the most common, and this will be the main grammatical point in this Unit. But as you may also want to know other alternatives, brief mention will be made in the

Expansión of other forms used when giving directions and instructions, for example the present tense, with which you are already familiar.

To ask for directions, for example *Where's the bank, please?*, *Can you tell me where the post office is?* or *Is this the road to Marbella?*, you will need to build on the grammar you already know from previous Units.

Have a look at these examples and their English translation before going on to the **Resumen gramatical**.

Asking and giving directions

¿Por dónde se va a la estación, por favor?
Which is the way to the station, please? (literally, *which way does one go to the station?*)
En la esquina puede doblar a la derecha. La estación está al final de la calle
You can turn right at the corner. The station is at the end of the street
¿Puede decirme dónde está Correos, por favor?
Can you tell me where the post office is, please?
Tiene que cruzar la calle y continuar hasta el primer semáforo. Correos está justo en la esquina
You have to cross the road and continue as far as the first set of traffic lights. The post office is right at the corner
¿Es ésta la carretera para Marbella?
Is this the road to Marbella?
Continúe por esta carretera hasta la estación de servicio y allí doble a la izquierda en dirección a Marbella
Continue along this road as far as the service station and turn left there towards Marbella
¿Dónde está el banco, por favor?
Where's the bank, please?
Coja la segunda calle a la derecha. El banco está al lado del ayuntamiento
Take the second street on the right. The bank is next to the town hall

Giving commands and instructions

Por favor cambie este dinero en el banco y regrese aquí
inmediatamente. Después llame a la señora Ardiles y dígale
que necesito verla urgentemente . . .

Please change this money at the bank and come back here
immediately. Then call señora Ardiles and tell her I need to see
her urgently . . .

Tome un comprimido cada dos horas

Take one tablet every two hours

Levante el auricular y espere el tono de marcar

Lift up the receiver and wait for the dialling tone

Resumen gramatical

1 Imperative

Uses
As stated in the **Nota preliminar**, the imperative is the form most
commonly associated with directions, commands and instructions.
Now study the formation of the imperative and consider again the
sentences under **Nota preliminar** and the further examples below.

Formation
In Spanish we use different imperative forms depending on who we
are talking to (polite or familiar) and whether we are speaking to one
or more than one person (singular or plural). To form the imperative
we use the stem of the 1st person singular of the present tense plus the
appropriate ending. Here are the polite imperatives of three regular
verbs representing each of the three conjugations: **doblar** (*to turn*),
responder (*to answer*), **subir** (*to go up*).

Present tense (1st person)	Imperative	
doblo	doble	*turn* (sing.)
	doblen	*turn* (pl.)

respondo	responda	*answer* (sing.)
	respondan	*answer* (pl.)
subo	suba	*go up* (sing.)
	suban	*go up* (pl.)

The negative imperative is formed by placing **no** before the verb: **no** doble (*don't turn*), **no** responda (*don't answer*), **no** suba (*don't go up*).

The following examples contain only regular verbs:

-ar

(doblar)	**Doble/n** a la derecha	*Turn left*
(continuar)	**Continúe/n** por esta calle	*Continue along this street*
(cambiar)	**Cambie/n** este dinero	*Change this money*

-er

(responder)	**Responda/n** a estas cartas	*Answer these letters*
(leer)	**Lea/n** las instrucciones	*Read the instructions*
(correr)	No **corra/n**	*Do not run*

-ir

(subir)	**Suba/n** al segundo piso	*Go up to the second floor*
(escribir)	**Escriba/n** al señor García	*Write to señor García*
(abrir)	**Abra/n** la puerta	*Open the door*

Nota: Observe that 1st conjugation verbs (**-ar**) acquire the endings of 2nd conjugation verbs (**-er**) while 2nd and 3rd conjugation verbs (**-er** and **-ir**) acquire the endings of the 1st conjugation.

The pronoun **Vd.** or **Vds.** is often added after the verb in order to soften the command:

doble Vd. a la izquierda   *turn left*
continúen Vds. por esta calle   *continue along this street*

Irregular imperative forms

As the imperative is formed with the stem of the 1st person singular of the present tense, verbs which are irregular in the present are also irregular in the imperative. This rule also applies to stem-changing verbs. Here are some examples:

Infinitive		Present	Imperative (sing./pl.)
seguir	(*to follow*)	sigo	siga/n
cerrar	(*to close*)	cierro	cierre/n
dar	(*to give*)	doy	dé/den
estar	(*to be*)	estoy	esté/n
hacer	(*to do, make*)	hago	haga/n
poner	(*to put*)	pongo	ponga/n
traer	(*to bring*)	traigo	traiga/n
volver	(*to return*)	vuelvo	vuelva/n
conducir	(*to drive*)	conduzco	conduzca/n
decir	(*to say*)	digo	diga/n
oír	(*to hear*)	oigo	oiga/n
salir	(*to go out*)	salgo	salga/n
seguir	(*to follow*)	sigo	siga/n
venir	(*to come*)	vengo	venga/n

Examples:

Venga/n mañana   *Come tomorrow*
Conduzca/n con cuidado   *Drive carefully*
No haga/n eso   *Don't do that*
Vuelva/n el martes   *Come back on Tuesday*
Cierre/n la puerta   *Close the door*

Ir, **saber** and *ser*

Ir (*to go*), **saber** (*to know*) and **ser** (*to be*) form the imperative in a different way.

Infinitive		Present	Imperative (sing./pl.)
ir	(*to go*)	voy	vaya/n
saber	(*to know*)	sé	sepa/n
ser	(*to be*)	soy	sea/n

Examples:

Vaya a la recepción	*Go to the reception*
Sépase que no lo haré otra vez	*Let it be known that I won't do it again*
Sean Vds. puntuales, por favor	*Be punctual, please*

Nota: Observe the passive **se** attached to the imperative form **sepa**. The addition of a syllable to the word requires the use of an accent in the third syllable from the end (see Pronouns with imperative below).

Spelling changes

Note the following spelling changes in verbs ending in **-car**, **-gar** and **-ger**:

Infinitive		Present	Imperative (sing./pl.)
buscar	(*to look for*)	busco	busque/n
tocar	(*touch, play*)	toco	toque/n
pagar	(*to pay*)	pago	pague/n
llegar	(*to arrive*)	llego	llegue/n
coger	(*to take, catch*)	cojo	coja/n

Examples:

Busque la llave	*Look for the key*
Pague Vd. ahora	*Pay now*
Por favor **lleguen** a la hora	*Please arrive on time*

Familiar imperatives

Familiar imperatives have different positive and negative forms.
Positive familiar forms:

Infinitive		Present	Imperative (sing./pl.)
doblar	(*to turn*)	doblo	dobla/d
responder	(*to answer*)	respondo	responde/d
subir	(*to go up*)	subo	sube/subid

Examples:

Dobla a la izquierda	*Turn left* (sing.)
Doblad a la derecha	*Turn right* (pl.)
Responde pronto	*Answer soon* (sing.)
Responded rápido	*Answer quickly* (pl.)
Sube al primer piso	*Go up to the first floor* (sing.)
Subid por esta calle	*Go up this road* (pl.)

Negative familiar forms:

Infinitive		Present	Imperative (sing./pl.)
doblar	(*to turn*)	doblo	no dobles
			no dobléis
responder	(*to answer*)	respondo	no respondas
			no respondáis
subir	(*to go up*)	subo	no subas
			no subáis

Examples:

No dobléis aquí, doblad en la esquina	*Do not turn here, turn at the corner* (pl.)
No respondas hoy, responde mañana	*Do not reply today, reply tomorrow* (sing.)

No subáis al primer piso,
    subid al segundo

Don't go up to the first floor,
    go up to the second (pl.)

Irregular familiar imperatives
The following verbs form the singular positive familiar imperative in
an irregular way.

decir	(*to say*)	di
hacer	(*to do, make*)	haz
ir	(*to go*)	ve
oír	(*to hear*)	oye
poner	(*to put*)	pon
salir	(*to go out*)	sal
ser	(*to be*)	sé
tener	(*to have*)	ten
venir	(*to come*)	ven

Examples:

Haz lo que digo
Ve inmediatamente
¡**Oye**!
¡**Sal** de aquí!
Ven aquí un momento

Do what I say
Go immediately
Listen!
Get out of here!
Come here a moment

Nota: Plural forms are regular.

Pronouns with imperative
If the imperative includes a pronoun, this must go at the end of the
positive form but before the negative one. Positive imperatives which
carry a pronoun may need to add an accent.

Examples:

Dígale que necesito verla
No **lo** traiga hoy

Tell her I need to see her
Do not bring it today

Tráigalo mañana	*Bring it tomorrow*
No lo haga así	*Don't do it like this*
Hágalo de esta manera	*Do it this way*
Llámame a las 6.00	*Call me at 6.00*

En contexto

1 *Asking the way.*

Turista   Buenas tardes. ¿Dónde está la oficina de turismo, por favor?

Policía   Está cerca de la estación. Siga Vd. todo recto por esta calle hasta el final, allí doble Vd. a la izquierda y continúe por esa misma calle hasta el segundo semáforo. La oficina de turismo está en la esquina.

Turista   Muchas gracias.

Policía   De nada.

siga Vd. todo recto	*go straight on*
por esta calle	*along this street*
esa misma calle	*that same street*
el semáforo	*traffic light*

2 *Giving instructions in the office.*

Jefe   Teresa, venga a mi despacho un momento, por favor.

Secretaria   Sí, ¿dígame?

Jefe   Mire, vaya al banco e ingrese estos cheques en mi cuenta corriente y después vaya a correos y eche estas cartas. Antes de volver pase por la papelería y tráigame el material de oficina que pedimos ayer. Ah, y pregunte en la agencia de viajes si está lista mi reserva para Santiago de Chile . . .

mire	*look*
ingrese (ingresar)	*deposit (to deposit)*
la cuenta corriente	*current account*
eche (echar) estas cartas	*post (to post) these letters*
pase por (pasar)	*stop by (to stop by)*
el material de oficina	*office material*
pedimos (pedir)	*we ordered (to order)*
pregunte (preguntar)	*ask (to ask)*
si está listo/a	*if it's ready*

Explicaciones

Because of their formal context, the polite imperative form has been used in both dialogues:

siga Vd. todo recto	*go straight on*
doble Vd. a la izquierda	*turn left*
vaya al banco	*go to the bank*
eche estas cartas	*post these letters*

In a familiar context, you would need to use the familiar imperative. Practise changing the formal imperatives in both dialogues into the familiar form, as if you were talking to a friend, for example **sigue todo recto** or **ve al banco**.

Expansión

1   Present tense used in giving directions

One simple but less frequent way of giving directions is by using the present tense (for its forms see Units 7 and 8). Examples:

¿Dónde está el museo, por favor?
Where's the museum, please?

Vd. continúa por esta calle hasta el semáforo y luego dobla a la
derecha. El museo está al lado de la catedral.
*You continue along this street as far as the traffic lights and then
you turn right. The museum is next to the cathedral.*
¿Puede decirme dónde hay un supermercado, por favor?
Can you tell me where there's a supermarket, please?
Vd. coge la tercera calle a la izquierda y sigue todo recto hasta
llegar a una pequeña plaza. Allí hay un supermercado.
*You take the third street on the left and you go straight on until you
reach a small square. There's a supermarket there*

2   Infinitive used in giving directions

Directions and instructions are sometimes given through the use of
infinitives. This is particularly common in the written language, for
example in notices, advertisements and generally in cases where the
language has to be kept simple and precise. Here are some examples:

No entrar	*Do not enter*
No aparcar	*Do not park*
No fumar	*Do not smoke*
Escribir al apartado 234	*Write to PO Box 234*
Tomar un comprimido antes de cada comida	*Take one tablet before each meal*

21 Expressing emotional reactions, possibility and doubt

Nota preliminar

In English, emotional reactions such as hope, fear, regret, satisfaction, annoyance, may be expressed through sentences like these:

Hope: *She hopes he answers her letter.*
Fear: *I fear they may not come back.*
Regret: *I'm sorry we can't accept the invitation.*
Satisfaction: *We're glad they're here.*
Annoyance: *It annoys me that you don't work.*

From the point of view of usage, what these sentences have in common is that they all express emotional reactions of some sort. From a grammatical point of view they are also similar: a main clause with a principal verb in the present tense (e.g. *she hopes, I fear*) is followed by another clause with a verb which is also in the present tense (e.g., *he answers her letter, they may not come back*). The linking word **that**, which is not obligatory, has been omitted. Compare: *she hopes **that** he answers her letter, she hopes he answers her letter*.

Possibility and doubt may be expressed in English through a similar construction, as may be seen from the examples below:

Possibility: *It's possible that they may get married.*
Possibility: *It's possible that we may travel to Spain.*
Doubt or uncertainty: *I don't think she'll sell the car.*
Doubt or uncertainty: *I doubt that he has the money.*

Spanish differs somewhat from English in the way it expresses these ideas. In the main clause there is no variation. The main verb may, as in English, be in the present tense or, depending on the type of verb and the context, in the past or the future (e.g., *I was glad he was there*, or *It'll be impossible for them to find us*), but the linking word **que** (*that*, in English), which introduces the second clause – called the subordinate clause – may not be omitted in Spanish. The main difference between the two languages lies in the verb in the subordinate clause. In Spanish, this second verb must be in the subjunctive.

The subjunctive mood covers a range of tenses – present subjunctive, imperfect subjunctive, perfect subjunctive, pluperfect subjunctive – which are different in form from all the ones we have covered so far in this book (for example, the present, preterite, imperfect tenses) and which we will now label as indicative tenses.

In the grammar notes below you will find information about the general use of the subjunctive in Spanish and about the present subjunctive in particular. Look at these examples and their English translation before going on to the **Resumen gramatical**.

Expressing emotional reactions

Ella espera que él responda
su carta

*She hopes that he answers
her letter*

Temo que no regresen	*I fear that they may not come back*
Siento que no podamos aceptar la invitación	*I'm sorry we can't accept the invitation*
Nos alegramos de que ellos estén aquí	*We're glad they're here*
Me molesta que no trabajes	*It annoys me that you don't work*

Expressing possibility

Es posible que se casen	*It's possible that they may get married*
Es posible que viajemos a España	*It's possible that we may travel to Spain*

Expressing doubt or uncertainty

No creo que ella venda el coche	*I don't think she'll sell the car*
Dudo que él tenga el dinero	*I doubt that he has the money*

Resumen gramatical

1   The subjunctive

General usage

(a) The subjunctive is generally associated with a subordinate clause introduced by **que** which is dependent on a main clause. The main clause usually carries the type of verb which calls for the use of the subjunctive in the subordinate clause, for example, verbs expressing emotion, possibility and doubt (see examples above).

(*b*) The subjunctive may also occur in relative clauses introduced by **que**, for example when the antecedent is not known, as in

Buscamos una secretaria que hable inglés	*We're looking for a secretary who speaks English*
Queremos una persona que conozca el oficio	*We want a person who knows the trade*

(*c*) The subjunctive is always used after certain subordinators, for example

para que (*so that*)
Le invitaré para que le veas	*I'll invite him so that you may see him*

en caso de que (*in case*)
En caso de que llegue dile que me espere	*In case he arrives tell him to wait*

con tal que (*as long as*)
Te lo contaré con tal que no se lo digas	*I'll tell you as long as you don't tell him*

(*d*) The subjunctive is found in main clauses containing commands or instructions (imperative form):

Venga aquí un momento, por favor	*Come here a moment, please*
No se lo diga	*Don't tell him*

(*e*) The idea of unreality or something which has not yet taken place is a common feature of many subjunctive clauses.

Se lo diré cuando llegue	*I'll tell him when he arrives*
Trabajaré hasta que termine	*I'll work until I finish*

For other uses of the subjunctive see Units 22 and 23.

2   Present subjunctive

Uses
The uses of the present subjunctive are no different from those of the subjunctive in general, as outlined above. The decision whether to use the present rather than some other subjunctive tense will depend largely on tense agreement and time reference. Although there is no strict rule about it, the present subjunctive normally occurs in sentences which carry a main clause in the present indicative, future or imperative. Examples:

Present indicative→present subjunctive

No creo que él esté allí   *I don't think he's there*

Future→present subjunctive

Será imposible que ellos nos   *It'll be impossible for them to*
visiten   *visit us*

Imperative→present subjunctive

Alégrate de que no sea nada   *You should be glad it's*
serio   *nothing serious* (literally,
                                    be glad . . .)

Formation
Like the imperative (see Unit 20) the present subjunctive is formed from the 1st person singular of the present indicative, e.g. **hablo** (**hablar**, *to speak*), **respondo** (**responder**, *to reply, answer*), **escribo** (**escribir**, *to write*). Drop the **-o** and add the corresponding endings: one set of endings for 1st conjugation verbs and another for the 2nd and 3rd conjugation. The 1st and 3rd person singular of the present subjunctive correspond in form to formal imperatives (see Unit 20).

hablar (*to speak*)	**responder** (*to reply*)	**escribir** (*to write*)
hable	responda	escriba
hables	respondas	escribas
hable	responda	escriba
hablemos	respondamos	escribamos
habléis	respondáis	escribáis
hablen	respondan	escriban

Examples:

With verbs expressing emotion:

Espero que ellos **hablen** español	*I hope they speak Spanish*
Me alegro de que ellos **trabajen** tan bien juntos	*I'm glad they work so well together*
Temo que ella no **comprenda**	*I'm afraid she may not understand*

With phrases indicating possibility:

Es posible que ellos no **respondan**	*It's possible that they may not answer*
Es probable que él nos **escriba**	*It's probable that he may write to us*
Puede ser que **regresen** por avión	*They may return by plane*

With verbs indicating doubt or uncertainty:

Dudamos que él nos **responda**	*We doubt that he will reply to us*
No creo que Carlos me **escriba**	*I don't think Carlos will write to me*

In independent clauses with words indicating doubt and possibility:

Quizá John **hable** con él mañana	*Perhaps John will speak to him tomorrow*
Tal vez ella **viaje** a Inglaterra .	*Perhaps she may travel to England*
Posiblemente se **queden** allí	*They may stay there*

Nota: If the clause with **creer** is in the affirmative, the verb in the subordinate clause will be an indicative verb. Compare these two sentences:

No creo que él me **llame**	*I don't think he'll call me*
Creo que él me **llamará**	*I think he'll call me*

Irregular forms of present subjunctive

As with imperatives, verbs which are irregular in the 1st person singular of the present indicative are also irregular in the present subjunctive. Here is an example:

Infinitive	Present indicative 1st person	Present subjunctive
decir (*to say, tell*)	digo	diga
		digas
		diga
		digamos
		digáis
		digan

Nota: For other examples of irregular forms refer to irregular imperatives in Unit 20.

As was the case with imperatives, some verbs are irregular in a different way:

dar (*to give*)	dé, des, dé, demos, deis, den
estar (*to be*)	esté, estés, esté, estemos, estéis, estén

haber (*to have*)	haya, hayas, haya,
	hayamos, hayáis, hayan
ir (*to go*)	vaya, vayas, vaya,
	vayamos, vayáis, vayan
saber (*to know*)	sepa, sepas, sepa,
	sepamos, sepáis, sepan
ser (*to be*)	sea, seas, sea,
	seamos, seáis, sean

Nota: The 1st and 3rd person singular of **dar** must carry an accent in order to distinguish them from the preposition **de**. The accents in the present subjunctive of **estar** are the same as in the present indicative: **estás, está, estáis, están**.

Examples:

Me alegro de que me lo **digas**	*I'm glad you're telling me*
Temo que él no lo **haga** bien	*I'm afraid he may not do it well*
Esperamos que ella lo **tenga**	*We hope she has it*
Dudo que Pedro **esté** allí	*I doubt that Pedro is there*
No creo que Enrique **vaya** a Granada	*I don't think Enrique will go to Granada*
Es posible que Elena **sepa** dónde está Carlos	*It's possible that Elena may know where Carlos is*
Espero que **sea** posible	*I hope it's possible*

En contexto

1 *An invitation to a birthday party.*

Felipe   Hola José Luis. Quiero invitarte a casa esta noche. Es el cumpleaños de Paloma.

José Luis   Lo siento, Felipe, pero no creo que pueda ir. Hoy

	llegan mis padres de Tenerife y tendré que ir al aeropuerto a recogerles.
Felipe	Es una lástima que no puedas venir. Posiblemente venga Francisco. Está en Madrid.
José Luis	Me alegro de que esté otra vez aquí. Espero verle otro día. Dile que me llame.
Felipe	Se lo diré. ¿Estarás en casa mañana?
José Luis	Tal vez salga un par de horas por la mañana, pero volveré antes del mediodía.
Felipe	Vale. Le diré a Francisco que te llame por la tarde.
José Luis	De acuerdo. Gracias.

a recogerles	*to pick them up*
es una lástima	*it's a pity*
otro día	*another day*
un par de horas	*a couple of hours*
antes del mediodía	*before midday*

2   *Read this extract from a letter.*

Querida Jane,

Hemos recibido tu carta y nos alegramos de que estés bien y tengas tanto éxito en tus estudios. Sentimos mucho que no puedas venir a Barcelona el próximo verano, pero esperamos que vengas para las Navidades. Es posible que Gonzalo también pase las Navidades con nosotros.¿Te acuerdas de él? Es aquel chico guapo que conocimos en Blanes ...

tanto éxito	*so much success*
¿te acuerdas de él?	*do you remember him?*
guapo	*good looking*
que conocimos (conocer)	*that we met (to meet, get to know)*

Explicaciones

Es una lástima que no
puedas venir

It's a pity you can't come

As a phrase indicating an emotional reaction (pity), **es una lástima** is followed by a subordinate clause with a subjunctive verb (**que no puedas venir**). Other phrases with similar meaning are **es una pena**, **¡qué pena!**. Here are two examples:

Es una pena que tengas que
marcharte

It's a pity you have to leave

¡Qué pena que el coche no
funcione!

*What a pity the car isn't
working!*

Expansión

1   Verbs and phrases denoting emotion

In the examples under **Nota preliminar** and in the **Resumen gramatical** you became familiar with the most common verbs and phrases associated with the expression of emotional reactions. The list below includes those as well as other verbs and phrases of this kind.

alegrarse	*to be glad*
escandalizarse	*to be shocked*
esperar	*to hope*
importar	*to mind*
horrorizarse	*to be shocked*
indignarse	*to be outraged*
molestarse	*to be annoyed*
sentir (e→ie)	*to be sorry*
sorprenderse	*to be surprised*
temer	*to fear*

es una lástima	it's a pity
es una pena	it's a pity
es una vergüenza	it's a shame
¡qué pena . . . !	what a pity!
¡qué lástima . . . !	what a pity!
¡qué vergüenza . . . !	what a shame!
¡qué rabia . . . !	what a nuisance!

Examples:

Me **sorprende** que digas eso	*I'm surprised you say that*
No me **importa** que él se marche	*I don't mind if he leaves*
Es una vergüenza que hagas esto	*It's a shame you did that*
¡Qué rabia que él no hable español!	*What a nuisance that he doesn't speak Spanish!*

2 Subjunctive or indicative

Certain words and phrases associated with the expression of possibility and doubt may be used equally with the indicative or the subjunctive, for example:

Quizá él habla español	
Quizá él hable español	*Perhaps he speaks Spanish*
Tal vez ella sepa dónde están	
Tal vez elle sabe dónde están	*Perhaps she knows where they are*

Nota: When **quizá** or **tal vez** come after the verb, this must be in the indicative form:

| El habla español **quizá** | *He speaks Spanish perhaps* |
| Ella sabe dónde están **tal vez** | *She knows where they are perhaps* |

A lo mejor (*perhaps*), a very frequent phrase in colloquial language, is always used with an indicative verb:

  A lo mejor lo haré   *Perhaps I'll do it*
  A lo mejor llegan esta tarde *Perhaps they arrive this*
              afternoon

Posiblemente (*probably*) is normally subjunctive, but it may also be used with the indicative:

  Posiblemente está en su   *He's probably in his office*
   despacho

3 Expressing emotional reactions, possibility and doubt with reference to the recent past

To express emotional reactions, possibility and doubt with reference to the past, as in *I hope he has found the money*, *It's possible that he may have found it* and *I don't think he has found it*, you need to use a present indicative verb in the main clause followed by a verb in the perfect subjunctive in the subordinate clause.

Perfect subjunctive
The perfect subjunctive is formed with the present subjunctive of **haber**, *to have* (**haya, hayas, haya, hayamos, hayáis, hayan**), followed by a past participle. Examples:

  Espero que él **haya**   *I hope he has found the*
   encontrado el dinero   *money*
  Es posible que lo **haya**   *It's possible that he may have*
   encontrado   *found it*
  No creo que lo haya
   encontrado   *I don't think he has found it*

22   Expressing wishes and orders

Nota preliminar

In English, wishes and preferences are expressed in a number of ways. With regard to yourself, you can simply say *I want to go, I prefer to do it, I don't wish to do it*, etc. With regard to other people you can use sentences such as *I want you to go, I'd prefer him to do it* and *I'd like her to do it*. A similar construction, but with a different tense, may be used with reference to the past: *they wanted me to help them* or *I wanted him to write*. The use of the infinitive (e.g. *to go, to do*) is a common feature of all these sentences, no matter whether they refer to yourself (e.g. *I want to go*) or to others (*I want you to go*). In Spanish, however, we can only use the infinitive if we are expressing personal wishes not involving others, for example **deseo ir** (*I wish to go*) and **él prefiere**

quedarse (*he prefers to stay*). But if those wishes or preferences are with regard to other people, then we need to use a construction consisting of a main clause with an indicative verb followed by a subordinate clause introduced by **que** and carrying a subjunctive verb. For example:

Quiero que tú vayas	*I want you to go*
Él prefiere que yo me quede	*he prefers me to stay*

The same rule above applies to indirect orders and commands such as:

Quiero que Vd. esté aquí a las 5.00	*I want you to be here at 5.00*
Insisto que lo haga	*I insist that you do it*

Tense agreement

Spanish also requires tense agreement between the verb in the main clause and the one in the subordinate clause. In Unit 21 we saw that a main clause verb in the present indicative, future and imperative will normally be followed by a present subjunctive in the subordinate clause (see page 184). But if the main verb is in the past (e.g. **yo quería**, *I wanted*) or the conditional (e.g. me gustaría, *I'd like*), tense agreement requires that the verb in the subordinate clause be not in the present but in the imperfect subjunctive. This point, among others, will be explained further in the grammar notes below.

Study these examples and their English translation before going on to the **Resumen gramatical**.

Expressing wishes and preferences with regard to other people

Referring to the present or future:

Quiero que me ayudes	*I want you to help me*
No quiero que vayas	*I don't want you to go*

¿Qué quieres que le diga?	*What do you want me to tell him?*
Prefiero que no le digas nada	*I'd prefer you not to tell him anything*
¿Dónde desea Vd. que lo dejemos?	*Where do you wish us to leave it?*
Quiero que lo dejen aquí	*I want you to leave it here*
Preferiría que él me llamara	*I'd prefer him to call me*
Me gustaría que tú hablaras con ella	*I'd like you to speak to her*

Referring to the past:

Ellos querían que yo les ayudara	*They wanted me to help them*
Marta quería que tú le escribieras	*Marta wanted you to write to her*
¿Qué querías que yo respondiera?	*What did you want me to reply?*
Quería que le contaras la verdad	*I wanted you to tell him the truth*

Expressing indirect orders

Referring to the present or future:

Quiero que vayas al banco	*I want you to go to the bank*
Le digo que no lo haga	*I'm telling you not to do it*
Él me ordena que trabaje más	*He orders me to work more*

Referring to the past:

Nos ordenaron que regresáramos	*They ordered us to return*
Les exigí que se marcharan	*I ordered them to leave*
Me obligaron a que no hablara	*They forced me not to speak*

Resumen gramatical

1 Imperfect subjunctive

Uses

As explained in the **Nota preliminar**, the expression of wishes and preferences involving other people and indirect commands require the use of a construction with a main clause carrying an indicative verb followed by a subordinate clause with a verb in the subjunctive. The decision whether to use the present, the imperfect or some other subjunctive tense will depend largely on tense agreement with regard to the verb in the main clause, and time reference.

The imperfect subjunctive normally occurs in sentences which carry a main clause in the imperfect, preterite or pluperfect, or else in the conditional (see 2 below) or the conditional perfect (see Unit 23). Here are some examples:

Imperfect indicative→imperfect subjunctive

Yo no quería que él se marchara	*I didn't want him to leave*

Preterite→imperfect subjunctive

Él no quiso que yo le llevara al aeropuerto	*He didn't want me to take him to the airport*

Pluperfect indicative→imperfect subjunctive

Ella nos había pedido que la llamáramos	*She had asked us to call her*

Conditional→imperfect subjunctive

Yo preferiría que os quedarais	*I'd prefer you to stay*

Conditional perfect→imperfect subjunctive

> Yo habría preferido que os   *I'd have preferred you to stay*
> quedarais

Now study the formation of the imperfect subjunctive and consider again the sentences under **Nota preliminar** and the further examples below.

The imperfect subjunctive can be formed in two ways. The first is directly derived from the third person plural of the preterite (see Unit 18). Here are some examples with regular verbs:

Infinitive		Preterite (3rd person pl.)	Imperfect subjunctive (1st and 3rd person sing.)
llegar	(*to arrive*)	llegaron	llegara
beber	(*to drink*)	bebieron	bebiera
subir	(*to go up*)	subieron	subiera

The same derivation occurs with irregular and stem-changing verbs:

poder	(*to be able to*)	pudieron	pudiera
estar	(*to be*)	estuvieron	estuviera
decir	(*to say*)	dijeron	dijera
ir/ser	(*to go/to be*)	fueron	fuera
traer	(*to bring*)	trajeron	trajera

Here is the imperfect subjunctive of three regular verbs representing each of the three conjugations: **llegar** (*to arrive*), **beber** (*to drink*) and **subir** (*to go up*). Note that **-er** and **-ir** verbs share the same endings:

llegar	beber	subir
llegara	bebiera	subiera
llegaras	bebieras	subieras
llegara	bebiera	subiera
llegáramos	bebiéramos	subiéramos
llegarais	bebierais	subierais
llegaran	bebieran	subieran

The imperfect subjunctive has a second set of endings which appear to be less frequent than the first. The two forms are generally interchangeable. Again, -er and -ir verbs share the same endings.

llegar	beber	subir
llegase	bebiese	subiese
llegases	bebieses	subieses
llegase	bebiese	subiese
llegásemos	bebiésemos	subiésemos
llegaseis	bebieseis	subieseis
llegasen	bebiesen	subiesen

Examples:

Expressing wishes and preferences with regard to other people

El quería que yo llegara/llegase a la hora	*He wanted me to arrive on time*
Ella prefería que yo no bebiera/bebiese	*She preferred me not to drink*
Roberto no deseaba que tú fueras/fueses	*Roberto didn't want you to go*
¿Qué querías que hiciéramos/hiciésemos?	*What did you want us to do?*
Yo quería que me ayudarais/ayudaseis	*I wanted you to help me*

Expressing orders in an indirect way

Nos ordenó que llegáramos/ llegásemos a la hora	*He ordered us to arrive on time*
Les ordené que subieran/ subiesen	*I ordered them to go up*
El jefe me exigió que trabajara/trabajase hasta las 6.00	*The boss ordered me to work until 6.00*

2 Conditional tense

Uses

The conditional tense is often used in sentences which express a wish or preference of some sort, for example:

Me gustaría que me escribieras/escribieses	*I'd like you to write to me*
Yo preferiría que él no viniera/viniese	*I'd prefer him not to come*

It is also generally used with verbs which express emotion (see Unit 21), for example:

Sentiría que ella no viniera/viniese	*I'd be sorry if she didn't come*
Me alegraría que lo hicieras/hicieses	*I'd be glad if you did it*
Sería una lástima que no le encontráramos	*It would be a pity if we didn't find him*

Formation

Like the future tense, the conditional is formed with the infinitive, to which the endings are added. The endings of the three conjugations are the same as those of the imperfect tense of **-er** and **-ir** verbs (see Unit 19). Here is the conditional tense of a regular verb:

preferir (*to prefer*)	
preferiría	*I'd prefer*
preferirías	*you'd prefer* (fam.)
preferiría	*you/he/she would prefer*
preferiríamos	*we would prefer*
preferiríais	*you would prefer* (fam.)
preferirían	*you/they would prefer*

Nota: The endings are exactly the same for **-ar** and **-er** verbs.

Examples:

Preferiría que no fueras/ fueses a Bogotá	*I'd prefer you not to go to Bogota*
Me gustaría que nos encontráramos/ encontrásemos en España	*I'd like us to meet in Spain*
Nos gustaría que tú nos acompañaras/ acompañases	*We'd like you to accompany us*

Irregular conditional forms

Verbs which have irregular stems in the future tense (see Unit 15) also have them in the conditional. The endings are the same as those of regular verbs. Here are some of the most common:

decir (*to stay*)	diría, dirías, diría, diríamos, diríais, dirían
haber (*to have*)	habría, habrías, habría, habríamos, habríais, habrían
hacer (*to do, make*)	haría, harías, haría, haríamos, haríais, harían
poder (*can, to be able*)	podría, podrías, podría, podríamos, podríais, podrían
poner (*to put*)	pondría, pondrías, pondría, pondríamos, pondríais, pondrían
querer (*to want*)	querría, querrías, querría, querríamos, querríais, querrían
saber (*to know*)	sabría, sabrías, sabría, sabríamos, sabríais, sabrían
salir (*to go out*)	saldría, saldrías, saldría, saldríamos, saldríais, saldrían
tener (*to have*)	tendría, tendrías, tendría, tendríamos, tendríais, tendrían
venir (*to come*)	vendría, vendrías, vendría, vendríamos, vendríais, vendrían

Nota: For a list of the most common irregular verbs in all tenses see pages 221–226 of **Apuntes gramaticales**.

Examples:

Yo no querría que él se marchara/marchase	*I wouldn't want him to leave*
¿Qué querrías que hiciera/ hiciese?	*What would you want me to do?*
Yo no sabría qué hacer	*I wouldn't know what to do*
Tú tendrías que trabajar más	*You'd have to work more*
¿Qué haríamos sin ti?	*What would we do without you?*

Nota: Because of the meanings of these irregular verbs, some of the examples do not correspond to the expression of wishes and indirect orders.

En contexto

1   *An invitation to the cinema.*

Antonio   Sara, me gustaría que me acompañaras al cine esta noche. Hay una película estupenda en el cine Capri.

Sara   Me encantaría ir contigo, pero desgraciadamente no puedo. Javier me pidió que fuera a su casa esta noche. Si no te importa, preferiría que lo dejáramos para mañana. Mañana por la noche estoy libre y podría acompañarte.

Antonio   De acuerdo. Hasta mañana, entonces.

me encantaría	*I'd love to*
desgraciadamente	*unfortunately*
si no te importa	*if you don't mind*
preferiría que lo dejáramos	*I'd prefer if we left it*

2 *Read this extract from a letter.*

Querida Soledad,

Cristóbal me pidió que te escribiera para reiterarte
nuestra invitación para este verano. Nos gustaría
mucho que pasaras estas vacaciones con nosotros.
Podríamos ir a Viña del Mar, como lo hicimos la
última vez que estuviste en Chile. ¿Te gustaría?

Mi jefe me ha dicho que tome mis vacaciones a partir
del 15 de enero, de manera que si estás libre entonces
puedes venirte de inmediato. Preferiría que me lo
confirmaras lo antes posible para hacer las reservas
de hotel.¿Qué te parece?

para reiterarte (reiterar)	*to reiterate*
como lo hicimos	*as we did*
la última vez	*last time*
a partir de	*starting on*
de manera que	*so*
de inmediato	*immediately*
lo antes posible	*as soon as possible*

Explicaciones

Javier me pidió que fuera a
su casa

*Javier asked me to go to his
house*

This sentence – denoting an indirect request – is grammatically the same as sentences like:

	Javier quería que fuera a su casa	*Javier wanted me to go to his place*
and		
	Javier me ordenó que fuera a su casa	*Javier ordered me to go to his house*

The three sentences only differ in their meaning or function. In the second text observe also the sentence:

Cristóbal me pidió que te escribiera	*Cristobal asked me to write to you*

Expansión

1 Verbs and phrases denoting wishes and preferences

In the examples under **Nota preliminar** and in the **Resumen gramatical** you became familiar with some verbs commonly associated with the expression of wishes and preferences, for example **querer** (e.g. **quiero que me lo digas**, *I want you to tell me*), **gustar** (**me gustaría que me llamaras**, *I'd like you to call me*), **preferir** (**preferiría que me escribieras**, *I'd prefer you to write to me*). Other less frequent verbs and phrases associated with the expression of wishes and preferences in the same context are the following:

encantar (*to like, love*)
Me encantaría que pasaras el Año Nuevo conmigo	*I'd love it if you'd spend the New Year with me*

Nota: **encantar** is conjugated like **gustar**.

agradar (*to like*)
Nos agradaría mucho que nos visitaran	*We'd very much like you to visit us*

Nota: **agradar** is conjugated like **gustar** and **encantar**.

sería bueno/estupendo/magnífico (*it would be good/great*)

Sería bueno que vinieras conmigo	*It would be good if you came with me*
Sería estupendo que nos encontráramos allí	*It would be great if we could meet there*

2 Verbs and phrases associated with orders

The verbs most frequently associated with the expression of indirect orders or commands are **ordenar** (e.g. **me ordenó que fuera**, *he ordered me to go*), **querer** (**quiero que esté aquí a las 4.00**, *I want you/him to be here at 4.00*). Other less frequent verbs associated with this particular language function are:

mandar (*to order*)

Me mandó que terminara el trabajo	*He ordered me to finish the work*

exigir (*to order, demand*)

Nos exigió que no dijéramos nada	*He ordered us not to tell anything*

obligar (*to force*)

Les obligó a que volvieran a España	*He forced them to return to Spain*

encargar (*to instruct*)

Nos encargaron que saliéramos temprano	*They instructed us to leave early*

23   Expressing conditions

Objetivos

In this Unit you will learn how to:

Express open conditions • Express remote conditions
• Express unfulfilled conditions

Contenido gramatical

'Si' in conditional sentences • Pluperfect subjunctive
• Perfect conditional • Pluperfect subjunctive for perfect
conditional in unfulfilled conditions • 'De' + infinitive to
express conditions • Phrases expressing conditions

Nota preliminar

To express conditions in Spanish we normally use the word **si** (*if*),
followed by an indicative tense in open conditions (e.g. *if I have time,
I'll go*) and by a subjunctive tense in remote conditions (e.g. *if I had
time, I'd go*) and unfulfilled conditions (e.g. *if I'd had time, I'd have
gone*). In the grammar section below you will find a detailed
explanation of the combination of tenses normally used to express the
different types of conditions.

Study these examples and their English translation before you go
on to the **Resumen gramatical**.

Expressing open conditions

Si tengo tiempo iré	*If I have time I'll go*
Si no llegan a la hora me voy	*If they don't arrive on time I'll go*

Expressing remote conditions

Si tuviera/tuviese tiempo iría	*If I had time I'd go*
Si lo supiera/supiese te lo diría	*If I knew I'd tell you*

Expressing unfulfilled conditions

Si hubiera/hubiese tenido tiempo habría/hubiera ido	*If I'd had time I'd have gone*
Si hubiéramos/hubiésemos estado aquí le habríamos/hubiéramos visto	*If we had been here, we'd have seen him*

Resumen gramatical

1 *Si* (if) in conditional sentences

In open conditions:

Si is the word most frequently used in Spanish when we want to express conditions. In open conditions, that is, conditions which may or may not be fulfilled, **si** is always followed by an indicative tense, with a tense pattern which is no different from English. Consider these examples and, again, the ones under **Nota preliminar**.

Si es como él dice es mejor no hacerlo. (**si** + present + present)	*If it is as he says it's better not to do it*

Si ella me escribe le responderé de inmediato. (si + present + future)	*If she writes to me I'll answer her right away*
Si has hecho tus deberes podrás salir. (si + perfect tense + future)	*If you've done your homework you'll be able to go out*
Si salieron a las 6.00 ya deben de estar en Caracas. (si + preterite + present)	*If they left at 6.00 they must already be in Caracas*

In remote conditions:

In remote conditions such as **si lloviera/lloviese no saldríamos** (*if it rained we wouldn't go out*), the **si** clause carries a verb in the imperfect subjunctive (see Unit 22) followed by a clause with a verb in the conditional. Here are some examples:

Imperfect subjunctive + conditional

Si fueras/fueses allí le verías	*If you went there you'd see him*
Si tomáramos/tomásemos un taxi llegaríamos a tiempo	*If we took a taxi we'd arrive on time*

Nota: The two examples above correspond to conditions which may be fulfilled. There is little difference between these conditions and the ones expressed in:

Si vas allí le verás	*If you go there you'll see him*
Si tomamos un taxi llegaremos a tiempo	*If we take a taxi we'll arrive on time*

Now consider these examples:

Si ella hablara/hablase inglés la contrataríamos	*If she spoke English we'd hire her*

Si él estuviera/estuviese aquí
te lo presentaría

*If he were here I'd introduce
him to you*

Nota: The examples above correspond to conditions which are contrary to fact:

ella no habla inglés
él no está aquí

she doesn't speak English
he's not here

The verb in the **si** clause here must necessarily be in the subjunctive.

Unfulfilled conditions:

In unfulfilled conditions such as **si hubiera/hubiese llovido no habríamos salido** (*if it had rained we wouldn't have gone out*), the **si** clause carries a verb in the pluperfect subjunctive followed by a clause with a verb in the perfect conditional (for a variant of this construction see **Expansión**).

Si ellos se hubieran/hubiesen
casado habrían sido
felices

Si Miguel me hubiera/
hubiese invitado yo
habría aceptado

*If they had married they'd
have been happy*

*If Miguel had invited me I'd
have accepted*

Nota: for the formation of the pluperfect subjunctive and the perfect conditional and further examples of conditional sentences see 2 and 3 below.

2   Pluperfect subjunctive

Usage

Apart from its specific use in unfulfilled conditions, the uses of the pluperfect subjunctive are, generally speaking, those of the subjunctive as a whole. It is normally found in subordinate clauses preceded by a main clause with a verb in the past, for example:

No creí que él hubiera   *I didn't think he had*
   tenido éxito   *succeeded*

But:

Creí que él había tenido   *I thought he had succeeded*
   éxito
Yo esperaba que ya   *I was hoping you had already*
   hubieras terminado   *finished*

Formation

The pluperfect subjunctive is formed with the imperfect subjunctive of
haber plus a past participle. Example:

	hubiera/hubiese ido		*I had gone . . .*
	hubieras/hubieses ido		*you had gone . . .* (fam.)
	hubiera/hubiese ido		*you/he/she had gone . . .*
Si	hubiéramos/hubiésemos ido	*If*	*we had gone . . .*
	hubierais/hubieseis ido		*you had gone . . .* (fam.)
	hubieran/hubiesen ido		*you/they had gone . . .*

Nota: The two endings are interchangeable.

Examples:

Si hubieras/hubieses ido a   *If you had gone to Seville*
   Sevilla te habría gustado   *you'd have liked it*
Si ellos hubieran/hubiesen   *If they had had money they'd*
   tenido dinero habrían   *have travelled*
   viajado

3 Perfect conditional

Usage

The most common use of the perfect conditional is in sentences which
refer to actions which could have taken place under certain
conditions, as in *If I had known he was here, I wouldn't have come.* Now

study the formation of the perfect subjunctive and then consider again the sentences under **Nota preliminar** (unfulfilled conditions) and the further examples below. (See also **Expansión**.)

Formation

The perfect conditional is formed with the conditional of **haber** followed by a past participle. Example:

habría estudiado	*I would have studied*
habrías estudiado	*you would have studied (fam.)*
habría estudiado	*you/he/she would have studied*
habríamos estudiado	*we would have studied*
habríais estudiado	*you would have studied (fam.)*
habrían estudiado	*you/they would have studied*

Examples:

Si yo hubiera/hubiese tenido el libro habría estudiado	*If I had had the book I would have studied*
Si ella hubiera/hubiese visto la película le habría gustado	*If she had seen the film she would have liked it*
Si yo hubiera/hubiese sabido que él estaba aquí no habría venido	*If I had known he was here I wouldn't have come*
Si hubiéramos/hubiésemos podido te habríamos ayudado	*If we had been able to we would have helped you*

En contexto

1 *If I had known . . .*

Ricardo   ¿Sabes que Julio estuvo aquí ayer?

Gonzalo	¡Qué lástima! Si lo hubiera sabido habría venido yo también. Hace mucho tiempo que no le veo.
Ricardo	Ahora está en casa de sus padres. Si quieres podemos llamarle.
Gonzalo	De acuerdo. ¿Tienes su número de teléfono?
Ricardo	Sí, espera un momento.

> **ayer**   *yesterday*

2 *If I had money . . .*

Edgardo	Alba ha decidido vender su piso. ¿Lo sabías?
Mónica	¡No me digas! Es un piso estupendo. Si tuviera dinero lo compraría. ¿Sabes en cuánto lo vende?
Edgardo	No lo sé, pero si te interesa puedo preguntárselo.
Mónica	Sí, me interesa mucho. Es un piso muy bonito y es bastante grande.
Edgardo	Se lo preguntaré.

ha decidido (decidir)	*she has decided*
¿lo sabías?	*did you know about it?*
¡no me digas!	*don't say!*
si te interesa	*if you are interested*
puedo preguntárselo	*I can ask her*

Explicaciones

1 Si te interesa . . . *If you are interested* . . . Literally, this phrase will translate into English as *If it interests you.* **Interesar**, a regular verb, is normally conjugated like **gustar** (e.g. **me interesa/n**, **te interesa/n**, **le interesa/n** . . .)

2 Notice the use of the direct object pronoun **lo** in **puedo**

preguntárselo (*I can ask her*) and **se lo preguntaré** (*I will ask her*). **Lo** here stands for *it*, that is, for what you are going to ask: *I can ask her about it, I will ask her about it*. In the phrase **no lo sé**, **lo** has a similar function: *I don't know it/about it*.

Expansión

1 Pluperfect subjunctive for perfect conditional in unfulfilled conditions

As explained in the **Resumen gramatical**, unfulfilled conditions are normally expressed through a **si** clause with a verb in the pluperfect subjunctive followed by a clause with a verb in the perfect conditional. In colloquial speech, however, the perfect conditional is sometimes replaced by the pluperfect subjunctive (the **-ra** form). The result is that you get the same tense in the **si** clause and in the main clause. Here are some examples:

> Si yo no hubiera/hubiese comido ese pescado no me hubiera (habría) enfermado
>
> *If I hadn't eaten that fish I wouldn't have become ill*
>
> Si Juan hubiera/hubiese sabido lo que pasó se hubiera (habría) enfadado
>
> *If Juan had known what happened he would have got angry*

2 *De* + infinitive to express conditions

Si + finite verb (e.g. **si yo lo hubiera/hubiese visto . . .** , *if I had seen it . . .*) may be replaced by **de** + infinitive (e.g. **de haberlo visto . . .**) when the verb in the **si** clause and the one in the subordinate clause both refer to the same person, for example:

> Si yo le hubiera/hubiese visto yo le habría/hubiera saludado. De haberle visto yo le habría/hubiera saludado
>
> *If I had seen him I would have greeted him*

Si ella hubiera/hubiese sabido que yo estaba aquí ella me habría/
hubiera llamado

De haber sabido que yo estaba aquí ella me habría/hubiera llamado	*If she had known I was here she would have called me*

Si es así, no hay nada más que hacer

De ser así, no hay nada más que hacer	*If it's like that, there's nothing more to be done*

3   Phrases expressing conditions

a menos que, a no ser que (*unless*)

No vendré mañana, **a menos que/a no ser que** tú me lo pidas	*I won't come tomorrow unless you ask me to*

a condición de que, con tal (de) que (*as long as*)

Te lo contaré **a condición de que/con tal (de) que** no se lo digas a nadie	*I'll tell you as long as you don't tell anybody*

por si (*in case*), **por si acaso** (*just in case*)

He comprado más carne **por si** José viene a cenar	*I've bought more meat in case José comes to dinner*
Cambiaré más dinero **por si acaso**	*I'll change some more money just in case*

Apuntes gramaticales
(Grammar notes)

These grammar notes include points not treated in the main part of the course as well as others which need to be expanded.

1 *Articles*

Use of the definite article (*el, la, los, las* – 'the')

(*a*) Before names of languages, unless they are preceded by the verb **hablar** or the preposition **en** (*in*).

    Me gusta **el** español   *I like Spanish*

(*b*) Before titles in general, for example **señor, señora, doctor**, except in direct address.

    El doctor Díaz y **la** señora   *Doctor Díaz and señora*
       Martínez están aquí   *Martínez are here*

(*c*) With parts of the body, instead of a possessive adjective.

    Me lavaré **las** manos   *I'll wash my hands*

(*d*) With days of the week.

    Él llega **el** lunes 15   *He's arriving on Monday 15th*

    (But: **Hoy es jueves**   *Today is Thursday*)

(*e*) Before the names of certain countries, although the general tendency nowadays is to omit it.

> **la** Argentina, **el** Perú, **el** Ecuador, **el** Brasil

(*f*) Before abstract nouns in general.

> **La** drogadicción es un problema serio
>
> *Drug addiction is a serious problem*

(*g*) Before words which indicate measure and weight.

> Cuesta 500 pesetas **el** kilo
>
> *It costs 500 pesetas a kilo*

(*h*) As a substitute for a noun.

> **El** coche de Paco es rojo y **el** de Ana también
>
> *Paco's car is red and so is Ana's*

Omission of the indefinite article (*un, una, unos, unas* – 'a', 'an', 'some')

(*a*) Before the names of professions and occupations.

> Soy médico
>
> *I'm a doctor*

(*b*) In certain set phrases which carry the verb **tener**.

> No tengo coche
>
> *I haven't got a car*
>
> Ella tiene fiebre
>
> *She has a fever*

(*c*) Before words like **cien**, **mil**, **otro**.

> Tengo cien/mil pesetas
>
> *I have a hundred/a thousand pesetas*
>
> ¿Tiene Vd. otro?
>
> *Have you got another one?*

(*d*) After words like **tal** (*such as*) and **que** (*what a*)

Hicieron tal ruido	*They made such a noise*
¡Qué pena!	*What a pity!*

The neuter article *lo*

This is used only with certain adjectives, adverbs and whole sentences, never with a noun.

No sabes **lo** hermoso que es	*You don't know how beautiful it is*
Lo mejor es no decir nada	*The best thing is not to say anything*
¿Recuerdas **lo** que te dije ayer?	*Do you remember what I told you yesterday?*

Contractions

(*a*) **a + el = al**

Voy a ir **al** cine	*I'm going to the cinema*

(*b*) **de + el = del**

Este es el coche **del** señor Moreno	*This is señor Moreno's car*

2   *Nouns*

Gender: (masculine/feminine)

The following endings correspond normally to masculine nouns, but there are many exceptions.

-o	el barco	*ship*
-e	el jefe	*boss*
-l	el sol	*sun*
-r	el amor	*love*
-n	el tren	*train*
-s	el mes	*month*

Also masculine are the names of mountains, rivers and seas (e.g. **el Pacífico**, *the Pacific*), days and seasons (e.g. **el verano**, *summer*), colours (**el verde**, *green*), substances (e.g. **el oro**, *gold*), languages (e.g. **el inglés**, *English*) and countries, except those ending in unstressed **-a**.

The following endings correspond normally to feminine nouns, but there are exceptions.

-a	la sala	*sitting room*
-dad	la ciudad	*city*
-z	la paz	*peace*
-ción	la nación	*nation*
-sión	la pasión	*passion*
-ud	la actitud	*attitude*

Special rules

(*a*) Nouns ending in **-ista** are invariable, e.g. **el** or **la dentista**, *dentist*.

(*b*) Most nouns which end in **-nte** are also invariable, e.g. **el** or **la estudiante**, *student*.

(*c*) Some nouns change meaning according to gender, e.g. **el policía** *policeman*, **la policía** *police*; **el capital** *capital* (money), **la capital** *capital* (city).

(*d*) Some nouns have different forms for each sex, e.g. **el padre** *father*, **la madre** *mother*; **el hombre** *man*, **la mujer** *woman*.

Number (singular/plural)

(*a*) Most nouns form the plural by adding **-s**.

la casa (*house*)   las casas (*houses*)

(*b*) Nouns which end in a consonant normally add **-es**.

el profesor (*teacher*) los profesores (*teachers*)

(*c*) Nouns which end in **-z** change **-z** to **-c** and add **-es**.

la nuez (*nut*) las nueces (*nuts*)

(*d*) The masculine plural of some nouns may be used to refer to members of both sexes.

el padre (*father*) los padres (*parents*)
el hermano (*brother*) los hermanos (*brothers and sisters*)

3 *Adjectives*

Comparative

Superiority:

Madrid es más grande que *Madrid is bigger than*
Barcelona *Barcelona*

Inferiority:

Mi coche es menos potente *My car is less powerful than*
que el tuyo *yours*

Equality:

Mi casa es tan bonita como *My house is as beautiful as*
la de ella *hers*

Superlative

Este tren es el más rápido   *This is the fastest train*
María es la más inteligente   *Maria is the most intelligent*

Irregular forms

bueno (*good*)	mejor (*better*)	el/la mejor (*the best*)
malo (*bad*)	peor (*worse*)	el/la peor (*the worst*)
joven (*young*)	menor (*younger*)	el/la menor (*the youngest*)
viejo (*old*)	mayor (*older*)	el/la mayor (*the oldest*)

Nota: mayor (*older*) can only be used with reference to people.

4   *Relative pronouns*

Que (who, that, which)

El chico **que** está allí es mi amigo   *The boy who's there is my friend*
El tren **que** va a Madrid es ése   *The train that/which is going to Madrid is that one*

Quien, quienes (who, after a preposition)

La persona con **quien** me viste es mi hermana   *The person with whom you saw me is my sister*

Lo que (what)

No sé **lo que** pasa   *I don't know what happens*
Lo que necesito es dinero   *What I need is money*

Cuyo/a, cuyos/as (**whose**)

Andrés Peréz, **cuyo** matrimonio tuvo lugar ayer, es un hombre famoso	*Andrés Pérez, whose wedding took place yesterday, is a famous man*

Nota: **cuyo** must agree in gender and number with the noun it refers to.

5 *Prepositions* por *and* para

Uses of *por*:

(*a*) In time phrases.

Él saldrá **por** la mañana	*He'll leave in the morning*

(*b*) With means of transport.

Viajaré **por** avión	*I'll travel by plane*

(*c*) To indicate movement through or along.

Pasaremos **por** Madrid	*We'll go through Madrid*
Continúe **por** esta calle	*Continue along this street*

(*d*) To refer to cost or price.

Pagué dos mil pesetas **por** él	*I paid two thousand pesetas for it*

(*e*) To denote reason or cause.

Lo hice **por** ti	*I did it for you*

(*f*) In phrases denoting measure or number.

> El viaja a España tres veces
> **por** año

> He travels to Spain three
> times a year

(*g*) With a pre-arranged time limit.

> Fue a Madrid **por** dos
> semanas

> He went to Madrid for two
> weeks

(*h*) In passive sentences with **ser** + past participle.

> Las naranjas fueron
> cortadas **por** los
> campesinos

> The oranges were cut by the
> farmers

Uses of *para*:

(*a*) To denote length of time.

> Quiero una habitación **para**
> dos noches

> I want a room for two nights

(*b*) With time phrases.

> Lo necesito **para** el jueves

> I need it for Thursday

(*c*) To denote direction.

> Salió **para** Barcelona

> He left for Barcelona

(*d*) To denote purpose.

> Te prestaré el libro **para** que
> lo leas

> I'll lend you the book so that
> you read it

(e) Before names and personal pronouns.

Para Ana es una alegría muy grande	*For Ana it's a great happiness*
Para mí un café, por favor	*Coffee for me, please*

(f) With words such as **muy, suficiente, bastante, demasiado**.

No hay bastante dinero **para** comprarlo	*There isn't enough money to buy it*
Es demasiado tarde **para** decírselo	*It's too late to tell him/her*

6 Irregular verbs

The following list includes only the most common irregular verbs. Only irregular forms are given (verbs marked with an asterisk are also stem-changing).

abrir (*to open*)	*past participle*: abierto
andar (*to walk*)	*preterite*: anduve, anduviste, anduvo, anduvimos, anduvisteis, anduvieron *imperfect subjunctive*: anduviese, anduvieses, anduviese, anduviésemos, anduvieseis, anduviesen; anduviera, anduvieras, etc.
caer (*to fall*)	*present indicative*. (yo) caigo *present subjunctive*: caiga, caigas, caiga, caigamos, caigais, caigan *present participle*: cayendo *preterite*: (él, ella, Vd.) cayó, (ellos, ellas, Vds.) cayeron *imperfect subjunctive*: cayese, cayeses, cayese, cayésemos, cayeseis, cayesen; cayera, cayeras, etc.

conducir	*present indicative*: (yo) conduzco
(*to drive*)	*present subjunctive*: conduzca, conduzcas, conduzca, conduzcamos, conduzcáis, conduzcan
	preterite: conduje, condujiste, condujo, condujimos, condujisteis, condujeron
	imperfect subjunctive: condujese, condujeses, condujese, condujésemos, condujeseis, condujesen; condujera, condujeras . . .
cubrir	*past participle*: cubierto
(*to cover*)	
dar	*present indicative*: (yo) doy
(*to give*)	*preterite*: di, diste, dio, dimos, disteis, dieron
	present subjunctive: dé, des, dé, demos, deis, den
	imperfect subjunctive: diese, dieses, diese, diésemos, dieseis, diesen; diera, dieras, etc.
decir*	*present indicative*: (yo) digo
(*to say*)	*present subjunctive*: diga, digas, diga, digamos, digais, digan
	preterite: dije, dijiste, dijo, dijimos, dijisteis, dijeron
	imperfect subjunctive: dijese, dijeses, dijese, dijésemos, dijeseis, dijesen; dijera, dijeras, etc.
	future: diré, dirás, dirá, diremos, diréis, dirán
	conditional: diría, dirías, diría, diríamos, diríais, dirían
	imperative (*familiar, singular*): di
	present participle: diciendo
	past participle: dicho
escribir	*past participle*: escrito
(*to write*)	
estar	*present indicative*: estoy, estás, está, estamos, estáis, están
(*to be*)	*present subjunctive*: esté, estés, esté, estemos, estéis, estén
	preterite: estuve, estuviste, estuvo, estuvimos, estuvisteis, estuvieron
	imperfect subjunctive: estuviese, estuvieses,

estuviese, estuviésemos, estuvieseis, estuviesen;
estuviera, estuvieras, etc.

imperative (familiar, singular): está

haber
(*to have*)
see compound tenses

hacer
(*to do, make*)
present indicative: (yo) hago
present subjunctive: haga, hagas, haga, hagamos,
hagáis, hagan
preterite: hice, hiciste, hizo, hicimos, hicisteis,
hicieron
imperfect subjunctive: hiciese, hicieses, hiciese,
hiciésemos, hicieseis, hiciesen; hiciera, hicieras,
etc.
future: haré, harás, hará, haremos, haréis, harán
conditional: haría, harías, haría, haríamos, haríais,
harian
imperative: (Vd.) haga, (tú) haz
past participle: hecho

ir
(*to go*)
present indicative: voy, vas, va, vamos, vais, van
present subjunctive: vaya, vayas, vaya, vayamos,
vayáis, vayan
imperfect: iba, ibas, iba, íbamos, ibais, iban
preterite: fui, fuiste, fue, fuimos, fuisteis, fueron
imperfect subjunctive: fuese, fueses, fuese,
fuésemos, fueseis, fuesen; fuera, fueras, etc.
imperative: (Vd.) vaya, (tú) ve
present participle: yendo

leer
(*to read*)
preterite: (él, ella, Vd.) leyó, (ellos, ellas, Vds.)
leyeron
imperfect subjunctive: leyese, leyeses, leyese,
leyésemos, leyeseis, leyesen; leyera, leyeras, etc.
present participle: leyendo

morir*
(*to die*)
past participle: muerto

oír
(*to hear*)
present indicative: oigo, oyes, oye, oímos, oís,
oyen
present subjunctive: oiga, oigas, oiga, oigamos,
oigais, oigan
preterite: (él, ella, Vd.) oyó, (ellos, ellas, Vds.)
oyeron

	imperfect subjunctive: oyese, oyeses, oyese, oyésemos, oyeseis, oyesen; oyera, oyeras, etc.
	imperative: (Vd.) oiga, (tú) oye
	present participle: oyendo
poder* (*to be able to, can*)	*preterite*: pude, pudiste, pudo, pudimos, pudisteis, pudieron
	imperfect subjunctive: pudiese, pudieses, pudiese, pudiésemos, pudieseis, pudiesen; pudiera, pudieras, etc.
	future: podré, podrás, podrá, podremos, podréis, podrán
	conditional: podría, podrías, podría, podríamos, podríais, podrían
	present participle: pudiendo
poner (*to put*)	*present indicative*: (yo) pongo
	present subjunctive: ponga, pongas, ponga, pongamos, pongáis, pongan
	preterite: puse, pusiste, puso, pusimos, pusisteis, pusieron
	imperfect subjunctive: pusiese, pusieses, pusiese, pusiésemos, pusieseis, pusiesen; pusiera, pusieras, etc.
	future: pondré, pondrás, pondrá, pondremos, pondréis, pondrán
	conditional: pondría, pondrías, pondría, pondríamos, pondríais, pondrían
	imperative: (Vd.) ponga, (tú) pon
	past participle: puesto
querer* (*to want*)	*preterite*: quise, quisiste, quiso, quisimos, quisisteis, quisieron
	imperfect subjunctive: quisiese, quisieses, quisiese, quisiésemos, quisieseis, quisiesen; quisiera, quisieras, etc.
	future: querré, querrás, querrá, querremos, querréis, querrán
	conditional: querría, querrías, querría, querrríamos, querríais, querrían
romper (*to break*)	*past participle*: roto

saber
(*to know*)
	present indicative: (yo) sé
	present subjunctive: sepa, sepas, sepa, sepamos,
	   sepáis, sepan
	preterite: supe, supiste, supo, supimos, supisteis,
	   supieron
	imperfect subjunctive: supiese, supieses, supiese,
	   supiésemos, supieseis, supiesen
	future: sabré, sabrás, sabrá, sabremos, sabréis,
	   sabrán
	conditional: sabría, sabrías, sabría, sabríamos,
	   sabríais, sabrían
	imperative: (Vd.) sepa

salir
(*to go out*)
	present indicative: (yo) salgo
	present subjunctive: salga, salgas, salga, salgamos,
	   salgáis, salgan
	future: saldré, saldrás, saldrá, saldremos, saldréis,
	   saldrán
	conditional: saldría, saldrías, saldría, saldríamos,
	   saldríais, saldrían
	imperative: (Vd.) salga, (tú) sal

ser
(*to be*)
	present indicative: soy, eres, es, somos, sois, son
	present subjunctive: sea, seas, sea, seamos, seais,
	   sean
	preterite: fui, fuiste, fue, fuimos, fuisteis, fueron
	imperfect subjunctive: fuese, fueses, fuese,
	   fuésemos, fueseis, fuesen; fuera, fueras, etc.
	imperfect indicative: era, eras, era, éramos, erais,
	   eran
	imperative: (Vd.) sea, (tú) sé

soltar (*to loosen*)	*past participle*: suelto

tener*
(*to have*)
	present indicative: (yo) tengo
	present subjunctive: tenga, tengas, tenga,
	   tengamos, tengáis, tengan
	preterite: tuve, tuviste, tuvo, tuvimos, tuvisteis,
	   tuvieron
	imperfect subjunctive: tuviese, tuvieses, tuviese,
	   tuviésemos, tuvieseis, tuviesen; tuviera, tuvieras,
	   etc.

	future: tendré, tendrás, tendrá, tendremos, tendréis, tendrán
	conditional: tendría, tendrías, tendría, tendríamos, tendríais, tendrían
	imperative: (Vd.) tenga, (tú) ten
traer	*present indicative*: (yo) traigo
(*to bring*)	*present subjunctive*: traiga, traigas, traiga, traigamos, traigais, traigan
	preterite: traje, trajiste, trajo, trajimos, trajisteis, trajeron
	imperfect subjunctive: trajese, trajeses, trajese, trajésemos, trajeseis, trajesen; trajera, trajeras, etc.
	imperative: (Vd.) traiga
	present participle: trayendo
venir*	*present indicative*: (yo) vengo
(*to come*)	*present subjunctive*: venga, vengas, venga, vengamos, vengáis, vengan
	preterite: vine, viniste, vino, vinimos, vinisteis, vinieron
	imperfect subjunctive: viniese, vinieses, viniese, viniésemos, vinieseis, viniesen; viniera, vinieras, etc.
	future: vendré, vendrás, vendrá, vendremos, vendréis, vendrán
	conditional: vendría, vendrías, vendría, vendríamos, vendríais, vendrían
	imperative: (Vd.) venga, (tú) ven
	present participle: viniendo
ver	*present indicative*: (yo) veo
(*to see*)	*present subjunctive*: vea, veas, vea, veamos, veais, vean
	imperfect indicative: veía, veías, veía, veíamos, veíais, veían
	imperative: (Vd.) vea
	past participle: visto
volver*	*past participle*: vuelto
(*to come back*)	

7 Ser *and* estar

Uses of *ser*:

(*a*) To give personal information such as who you are, nationality, where you are from, occupation, marital status, religion, political affiliation.

Ella **es** Marta Paredes	*She's Marta Paredes*
Es española	*She's Spanish*
Es de Madrid	*She's from Madrid*

(*b*) To denote characteristics which are considered universal or part of someone's nature.

La Tierra **es** redonda	*The Earth is round*
Silvia **es** inteligente	*Silvia is intelligent*

(*c*) With time phrases.

¿Qué hora **es**?	*What time is it?*
La fiesta **es** a las 2.00	*The party is at 2.00*

(*d*) To refer to the material something is made of.

El bolso **es** de plástico	*The bag is made of plastic*

(*e*) To denote possession.

Ese libro **es** mío	*That book is mine*

(*f*) To denote cost.

¿Cuánto **es**?	*How much is it?*
Son 3.000 libras	*It's 3000 pounds*

(*g*) To indicate where an event will take place.

La manifestación **será** en la plaza	*The demonstration will be in the square*

(*h*) With impersonal expressions such as **es posible/imposible, es mejor, es conveniente, es difícil**.

> **Es posible** que él regrese   *It's possible that he may*
> pronto   *return soon*

(*i*) In passive constructions followed by a past participle.

> El niño **fue** secuestrado   *The child was kidnapped*

(*j*) With a noun complement, e.g. in identification.

> **Es** un ordenador   *It's a computer*

Uses of *estar*

(*a*) To denote a temporary state or condition.

> Hoy **está** muy bonita   *She looks very pretty today*

(*b*) To indicate position.

> Perú **está** en Sudamérica   *Peru is in South America*

(*c*) To denote marital status (see also **ser**).

> ¿**Estás** soltero o casado?   *Are you single or married?*

(*d*) To denote the result of a process.

> Los chicos **están** muy   *The children are very big*
> grandes

(*e*) To denote cost when there is regular variation, as with foreign currency.

> ¿A cuánto **está** el dólar?   *What's the rate for the*
>   *dollar? (literally, how*
>   *much is the dollar?)*

(*f*) Before a past participle to denote a condition resulting from an action.

La ventana **está** abierta   *The window is open*

(*g*) Before a gerund in continuous tenses, e.g. present continuous.

¿Qué **estás** haciendo?   *What are you doing?*

(*h*) To refer to a state of mind or health.

Carlos **está** contento   *Carlos is happy*
Luisa **está** enferma   *Luisa is ill*
¿Cómo **estás**?   *How are you?*

8 *Government of verbs*

Finite verb + infinitive

(*a*) With verbs denoting wants and likes, e.g. **querer** (*to want*), **preferir** (*to prefer*), **desear** (*to wish*), **gustar** (*to like*).

Quiero ir   *I want to go*
Me gusta venir aquí   *I like to come here*

(*b*) With verbs denoting ability and capacity, e.g. **poder** (*to be able to, can*), **saber** (*to know how to*).

No puedo hacerlo   *I can't do it*
Ella no sabe nadar   *She doesn't know how to swim*

(*c*) Certain verbs are always used with an infinitive, e.g.

acabar de   *to have just*
acostumbrar a   *to be in the habit of*

deber	*must, to have to*
dejar de	*to give up, stop*
empezar and **comenzar a**	*to begin, start*
enseñar a	*to teach to*
ir a	*to be going to*
ofrecer	*to offer*
soler	*to be in the habit of*
tener que	*to have to*

Acabo de llegar	*I have just arrived*
Tiene mucho que hacer	*He has a lot to do*
Dejaré de fumar	*I'll give up smoking*

(*d*) With verbs of perception, e.g. **ver** (*to see*), **oír** (*to hear*).

Le vi salir	*I saw him go out*
La oí entrar	*I heard her come in*

Nota: The infinitive is not normally used in constructions with a main clause and a subordinate clause, where the subjects of the main clause and the subordinate clause refer to different persons or things. Compare the following:

Él quiere que yo le ayude	*He wants me to help him*
Él quiere ayudarme	*He wants to help me*
Espero que tú viajes a España	*I hope you travel to Spain*
Espero viajar a España	*I hope to travel to Spain*

Finite verb + gerund

(*a*) With verbs of perception, particularly with **ver**.

Le vi pintando	*I saw him painting*
Me vieron trabajando	*They saw me working*

Nota: The gerund in this construction denotes an action still in progress. If the action is complete, we would use an infinitive:

Le vi **pintar**	*I saw him paint*

(*b*) With **seguir** and **continuar** (*to continue, go on*).

    Continuaremos andando   *We'll continue walking*
    Siguieron discutiendo   *They went on arguing*

or with **estar** to indicate an action in progress

    Estoy escribiendo   *I'm writing*
    Están hablando   *They're speaking*

(*c*) With **llevar** followed by a time expression to denote *for*.

    Llevan un año trabajando   *They've been working here*
      aquí   *for a year*
    Llevo mucho tiempo   *I've been waiting for a long*
      esperando   *time*

(*d*) With **andar**, in expressions denoting the idea of 'going round doing something'.

    Siempre **anda**   *He's always going round*
      interrumpiendo el trabajo   *interrupting other people's*
      de los demás   *work*
    Ella **anda** diciendo que nadie   *She's going round saying that*
      la quiere   *nobody loves her*

(*e*) With **quedarse**, in expressions denoting 'to remain doing something'.

    Me **quedé** observándola   *I stood watching her*
    Nos **quedamos** mirándoles   *We remained looking at them*

(*f*) With **acabar** (*to end up by*).

    Acabaron casándose   *They ended up getting*
                               married
    Acabó divorciándose   *He ended up getting divorced*

(*g*) With **venir**, to denote an action which started in the past and which is still valid or in progress.

Esto **viene** sucediendo desde hace mucho tiempo	*This has been happening for a long time*
Vengo diciéndotelo desde hace largo rato	*I've been telling you this for a long while*

(*h*) With **ir**, to refer to an action which is taking place gradually.

La situación **va** cambiando poco a poco	*The situation is changing little by little*
El barco **fue** despareciendo en el horizonte	*The boat slowly disappeared on the horizon*

Finite verb + past participle

(*a*) With **haber**, in perfect tenses.

He terminado	*I have finished*
¿Qué **has** hecho?	*What have you done?*

(*b*) With **estar**, to denote a state which is the result of an action.

El trabajo **está** terminado	*The work is finished*
La carta ya **está** escrita	*The letter is already written*

Nota: The past participle here agrees in number and gender with the noun it refers to.

9   *Stress, accentuation and spelling*

Stress and accentuation

(*a*) Words which end in a vowel, **n** or **s** stress the last syllable but one.

nada	*nothing*	ingeniero	*engineer*
toman	*they take*	chicos	*boys*

(b) Words which end in a consonant other than **n** or **s**, stress the last syllable.

feliz	*happy*	español	*Spanish*
Madrid	*Madrid*	mejor	*better*

(c) Words which do not follow the above rules, carry a written accent over the stressed syllable.

túnel	*tunnel*	allí	*there*
inglés	*English*	autobús	*bus*
invitación	*invitation*	teléfono	*telephone*

(d) Differences in meaning between certain similar words are shown through the use of an accent.

sí	*yes*	si	*if*
él	*he*	el	*the* (masc.)
sé	*I know*	se	*himself, herself*
mí	*me*	mi	*my*
dé	*give*	de	*of, from*

Question words carry an accent, and are preceded by an inverted question mark.

¿dónde?	*where?*	¿cuándo?	*when?*
¿qué?	*what?*	¿cómo?	*how?*

Spelling

Note the following changes in spelling.

(a) Nouns and adjectives which finish in **z** change the **z** into **c** to form the plural.

pez	*fish* (singular)	peces	*fish* (plural)
feliz	*happy*	felices	*happy*

(*b*) Some verbs may change their spelling in certain forms in order to keep the same sound of the infinitive.

llegar	*to arrive*	but llegué	*I arrived*
coger	*to catch*	but cojo	*I catch*
tocar	*to touch*	but toqué	*I touched*
sacar	*to take out*	but saqué	*I took out*

(*c*) A spelling change may also occur because of an accent in the infinitive or because there would otherwise be more than two vowels together.

caer *to fall*→cayó *he/she/it fell*→cayeron *you/they fell*
leer *to read*→leyó *he/she read*→leyeron *you/they read*
oír *to hear*→oyó *he/she/it heard*→oyeron *you/they heard*

(*d*) Notice also how **oír** *to hear* changes in the present tense.

oyes *you hear* (familiar)→oye *he/she/it hears*→oyen *you/they hear*

(*e*) Adjectives which end in **-ble** change **-ble** into **-bil** before adding the suffix **-ísimo** (see Unit 3).

| amable | *kind* | amabilísimo | *very kind* |
| notable | *notable* | notabilísimo | *very notable* |

Spanish–English Vocabulary

abajo *downstairs*
abogado (m.) *lawyer*
abuelos (m. pl.) *grandparents*
aburrido *boring*
acabar de *to have just*
aceptar *to accept*
acercarse *to approach, come near*
acompañar *to accompany*
acostarse *to go to bed*
acostumbrar a *to be in the habit of*
acuerdo: de— *all right*
además *besides*
aeropuerto (m.) *airport*
agencia (f.) *agency*
agencia de viajes (f.) *travel agency*
ahora *now*
ahora mismo *right now*
alegrarse *to be glad*
algo *something, anything*
alguien *somebody, anybody*
alguna vez *ever*
alguno *some, any*
allí *there*
almorzar *to have lunch*
alquilar *to rent*
alquiler (m.) *rent*
alto *tall*
amable *kind*
amigo (m.) *friend*
andaluz *Andalusian*
antes *before*; lo — posible *as soon as possible*
año (m.) *year*

año pasado (m.) *last year*
Año Nuevo (m.) *New Year*
aparcamiento (m.) *car park*
aparcar *to park*
apartamento (m.) *apartment*
aprender *to learn*
aquí *here*
argentino *Argentinian*
arriba *upstairs*
arte (f.) *art*
artículo (m.) *article*
asistir *to attend*
asuntos exteriores (m. pl.) *foreign affairs*
atardecer (m.) *evening, dusk*
atender *to look after*
aunque *although*
auricular (m.) *receiver*
autoridad (f.) *authority*
avión (m.) *aeroplane*
ayer *yesterday*
ayudar *to help*
ayuntamiento (m.) *town hall*
azul *blue*

bailar *to dance*
bajar *to go down*
bajo *short*
banco (m.) *bank*
baño (m.) *bathroom*
barato *cheap*
barrio (m.) *district*
bastante *quite, enough*
beber *to drink*

biblioteca (f.) *library*
bicicleta (f.) *bicycle*
bien *well, good*
billete (m.) *ticket*
blanco *white*
blusa (f.) *blouse*
bolígrafo (m.) *ball-point pen*
bolso (m.) *bag, handbag*
bonito *pretty*
botella (f.) *bottle*
británico *British*
bueno *good, well*
buenos días *good morning*
buscar *to fetch, come for, look for*

cabeza (f.) *head*
caer *to fall*
caja (f.) *case*
cajero automático (m.) *cash point*
calentar *to heat*
caliente *hot*
calor (m.) *heat*: hace — *it's warm, hot*
caluroso *hot (weather)*
calle (f.) *street*
cama (f.) *bed*
camarero (m.) *waiter*
cambio (m.) *change*
camino (m.) *way*
camisa (f.) *shirt*
campesino (m.) *farmer*
campo (m.) *country, countryside*
carne (f.) *meat*
carnicería (f.) *butcher's*
caro *expensive*
carretera (f.) *highway, main road*
carta (f.) *letter*
casa (f.) *house*
casado *married*
caso: en ese — *in that case*
catedral (f.) *cathedral*
católico *catholic*

cebolla (f.) *onion*
cena (f.) *dinner*
centro (m.) *centre*
centro deportivo (m.) *sports centre*
cine (m.) *cinema*
cita (f.) *appointment*
ciudad (f.) *city*
clima (m.) *climate*
cocina (f.) *kitchen*
cocinar *to cook*
coche (m.) *car*
coger *to take, catch*
colegio (m.) *school*
colombiano *Colombian*
color (m.) *colour*
comedor (m.) *dining room*
comer *to eat*
comida (f.) *food, lunch*
cómo *how*
cómo no *certainly*
cómodo *comfortable*
compartir *to share*
comprar *to buy*
comprimido (m.) *tablet*
conducir *to drive*
conmigo *with me*
conocer *to know, meet*
conseguir *to get*
considerar *to consider, think*
contaminado *polluted*
contar *to tell*
contar con *to have*
contigo *with you*
continuar *to continue*
contratar *to hire*
conversaciones (f. pl.) *talks*
copa (f.) *drink*
corbata (f.) *tie*
correos (m.) *post office*
correspondencia (f.) *mail*
cortar *to cut*

creer *to think*
cruzar *to cross*
cuál *which, what*
cuánto/s *how much/many*
cuarto de baño (f.) *bathroom*
cucharadita (f.) *teaspoonful*
cuenta (f.) *bill*
cuenta corriente (f.) *current account*
cumpleaños (f.) *birthday*
curso (f.) *course*
chaqueta (f.) *jacket*
chico (m.) *boy*
chileno *Chilean*
chuleta de cerdo (f.) *pork shop*

dar *to give*
datos personales (m. pl.) *personal information*
de *of, from*
deber *to have to, must*
deberes (m.pl.) *homework*
decir *to say, tell*
dejar *to leave*
de nada *you're welcome*
delgado *thin*
dentro *within, inside*
dependiente (m.) *shop assistant*
deporte (m.) *sport*
derecha: a la — *on the right*
desayunar *to have breakfast*
descansar *to rest*
desde *from*
desgraciadamente *unfortunately*
despacho (m.) *study, office*
despertar *to wake up*
después *afterwards*
día (m.) *day*
difícil *difficult*
dinero (m.) *money*
dirección (f.) *address*: en — a *towards*

disponer de *to have*
distancia (f.) *distance*
distinto *different*
doblar *to turn*
doble *double*
domingo *Sunday*
dormir *to sleep*
ducharse *to shower*
dudar *to doubt*
durante *during*

echar una carta *to post a letter*
edificio (m.) *building*
ejemplo (m.) *example*
encantar *to like, love*
encontrar *to find*
encontrarse *to meet, be, be situated*
enfadarse *to get annoyed*
enfermarse *to become ill*
enfrente *opposite*
ensalada (f.) *salad*
enseñar *to teach*
entonces *then*
entrada (f.) *entrance*
entrevistarse *to have talks*
enviar *to send*
equipaje (f.) *luggage*
escocés *Scottish*
escritorio (m.) *desk*
escuchar *to listen*
escuela (f.) *school*
esfuerzo (m.) *effort*
espacio (m.) *space*
español *Spanish*
esperar *to wait, hope, expect*
esquiar *to ski*
esquina (f.) *corner*
estación (f.) *station*; — de servicio *service station*
estar *to be*
estrella (f.) *star*

estudiante (m./f.) *student*
estudiar *to study*
estupendo *great, fantastic*
exigir *to demand*
existir *to exist*
éxito *success*
expedir *to dispatch*
exterior *facing the street*
extranjero *foreign:* (m.) *foreigner*

fábrica (f.) *factory*
fabricar *to manufacture*
fácil *easy*
factura (f.) *invoice, bill*
falda (f.) *skirt*
faltar *to miss, be absent*
familia (f.) *family*
farmacia (f.) *chemist's*
fecha (f.) *date*
feliz *happy*
fijo *fixed*
final: al — de *at the end of*
finales: a — de *at the end of*
fin de semana (f.) *weekend*
fino *good*
firma (f.) *firm, company*
formulario (m.) *form*
fotografía (f.) *photograph*
freir *to fry*
frío *cold*
frito *fried*
fruta (m.) *fruit*
fuego (m.) *light*
fuera *out, outside*
fumar *to smoke*

gafas (f. pl.) *glasses*
galleta (f.) *biscuit*
ganar *to earn*
gasolinera (f.) *petrol station*
gente (f.) *people*
gerente (m./f.) *manager*

gobierno (m.) *government*
gordo *fat*
gótico *gothic*
gracias *thank you*
gran *big, large, great*
grande *big, large*
guapo *goodlooking, pretty*
guía (m./f.) *guide (person)*
gustar *to like*

habitación (f.) *room*
hablar *to speak*
hacer *to do, make*
hacer falta *to need*
hallarse *to be situated*
hambre (f.) *hunger*
hasta *until, as far as*
hay que *one has to*
hermano (m.) *brother*
hervir *to boil*
hijo (m.) *son*
hindú *Indian*
hola *hello*
hombre (m.) *man*
hora (f.) *hour;* a la — *on time*
horario de trabajo (m.) *working hours*
húmedo *wet (climate)*

iglesia (f.) *church*
imaginar *to imagine*
importar *to mind*
indicar *to indicate*
individual *single*
inglés *English*
iniciar *to start, begin*
inmediato: de — *right away*
instalar *to install, establish*
instituto (m.) *school*
interesar *to interest*
interior *at the back*

invitado (m.) *guest*: — de honor *guest of honour*
irlandés *Irish*
irse *to leave*
izquierda: a la — *on the left*

jardín (m.) *garden*
jefe (m.) *manager, boss, head*
jefe de gobierno (m.) *head of government*
jefe de ventas (m.) *sales manager*
jugar *to play*
juntos *together*

lado: al — de *next to*
lana (f.) *wool*
largo *long*
lástima (f.) *pity*
lavarse *to wash oneself*
leer *to read*
lejos *far*
levantar *to lift*
levantarse *to get up*
libre *free*
libro (m.) *book*
limpio *clear*
listo *ready*
luego *then*
lugar (m.) *place*
lunes *Monday*
luz (f.) *light*
llamada (f.) *call*
llamar *to call*
llamarse *to be called*
llave (f.) *key*
llegar *to arrive*
llevar *to carry*: — + gerund *to have been doing something*
llover *to rain*
lluvia (f.) *rain*

madera (f.) *wood*
maleta (f.) *suitcase*

maletín (m.) *small suitcase*
malo *bad*
manzana (f.) *block; apple*
manera: de — que *so that*: de esta — *in this way*
mano (f.) *hand*
mañana *tomorrow*; (f.) *morning*
marcharse *to leave*
marido (m.) *husband*
marrón (m.) *brown*
más *more, else*
más o menos *more or less*
material de oficina (m.) *office material*
mayor *elderly*
medicina (f.) *medicine*
médico (m.) *doctor*
mediodía (m.) *midday*
mejor *better*; a lo — *perhaps*
mentira (f.) *lie*
menudo: a — *often*
mercado (m.) *market*
mes (m.) *month*
mesa (f.) *table*
mexicano *Mexican*
mientras *while, whilst*
ministro (m.) *minister*
minuto (m.) *minute*
molestarse *to be annoyed*
moneda (f.) *currency*
moreno *tanned*
morir *to die*
motivo (m.) *reason*
muchacho (m.) *boy*
mucho *much, a lot*; — gusto *pleased to meet you*
muerto *dead*
mujer (f.) *woman, wife*
museo (m.) *museum*
muy *very*

nacer *to be born*
nada *nothing*

nadar *to swim*
nadie *nobody*
naranja (f.) *orange*
Navidades (f. pl.) *Christmas*
necesitar *to need*
ninguno *none, any*
niño (m.) *child*
noche (f.) *night*
normalmente *normally*
norte (m.) *north*
noticia (f.) *news*
nuevamente *again*
nuevo *new*
número (m.) *number*

obligar *to force*
obtener *to obtain*
ocupado *busy*
ocupar *to occupy*
ocurrir *to happen*
oferta (f.) *offer*; en — *special offer*
oficina (f.) *office*
oficio (m.) *trade*
oír *to hear*
ojo (m.) *eye*
opinar *to think*
orden (m.) *order, kind*
ordenador (m.) *computer*
ordenar *to order*
oro (m.) *gold*
otra vez *again*
otro *other, another*

pagar *to pay*
país (m.) *country*
pan (m.) *bread*
panadería (f.) *baker's*
pantalones (m. pl.) *trousers*
papelería (f.) *stationer's*
paquete (m.) *parcel, package*
par (m.) *pair*
para *for, in order to*

parecer *to seem*
pariente (m.) *relative*
pasado *last, past*; —
    mañana *the day after tomorrow*
pasar *to come in, come by, spend (time)*
pasarlo bien *to have a good time*
paseo (m.) *walk*
película (f.) *film*
peluquería (f.) *hairdresser's*
pensar *to think*
perdonar *to forgive*
perdone *excuse me*
periódico (m.) *newspaper*
permiso de trabajo (m.) *work permit*
perro (m.) *dog*
persona (f.) *person*
personalmente *personally*
pertenecer *to belong*
peruano *Peruvian*
pescado (m.) *fish*
piscina (f.) *swimming pool*
piso (m.) *flat*
plancha: a la — *grilled*
playa (f.) *beach*
pobre *poor*
poco *little*
poder *to be able to, can*
pollo (m.) *chicken*
poner *to put*
por *for, by, per at*; — aquí *this way*
por favor *please*
portero (m.) *porter*
precio (m.) *price*
precioso *beautiful*
preguntar *to ask*
preocupado *worried*
preocuparse *to worry*
preparar *to prepare*
presentar *to introduce*
primero *first*

primo (m.) *cousin*
príncipe (m.) *prince*
privado *private*
probarse *to try on*
problema (m.) *problem*
producir *to produce*
profesor (m.) *teacher*
propiedad (f.) *property*
propio *own*
próximo *next*
pueblo (m.) *town, village*
puerta (f.) *door*
puerto (m.) *port*
pues *well, then, because*
qué *what, which*; ¿— tal? *how are you*
quedarse *to stay*
quejarse *to complain*
querer *to want, love*
quién *who*
quitarse *to take off* (clothes)
quizá *perhaps*

raro *strange*
rato (m.) *while, moment*
razón (f.) *reason*; tener — *to be right*
recado (m.) *message*
recibir *to receive*
recoger *to pick up*
recto *straight*; todo — *straight on*
redondo *round*
regresar *to return*
reiterar *to reiterate*
rellenar *to fill in*
reparar *to repair*
reserva (f.) *reservation*
resfriado: estar — *to have a cold*
reunión (f.) *meeting*
revista (f.) *magazine*
rico *rich*

robo (m.) *theft*
rojo *red*
ruido (m.) *noise*
ruidoso *noisy*

sábado *Saturday*
saber *to know, know how to*
sabroso *tasty*
sacar *to get, buy* (tickets)
sal (f.) *salt*
saludar *to greet*
secretaria (f.) *secretary*
seguir *to follow, continue*
segundo *second*
seguro: estar — *to be sure; sure, certain*
semáforo (m.) *traffic light*
semana (f.) *week*
sentir *to be sorry*
señor (m.) *Mr, sir, gentleman*
señora (f.) *Mrs, madam, lady*
señorita (f.) *Miss, young lady*
ser *to be*
servicios (m. pl.) *toilets*
siempre *always*
sierra (f.) *mountain*
simpático *nice*
socialista *socialist*
solamente *only*
soler *to be in the habit of, to usually*
solicitar *to request*
solicitud (f.) *application form*
sólo *alone*
sólo *only*
soltero *single*
sonar *to ring*
sopa de verduras (f.) *vegetable soup*
sostener *to hold*
suceder *to happen*
sucio *dirty*

supermercado (m.) *supermarket*
supuesto: por — *of course, certainly*

talla (f.) *size (clothes)*
tal vez *perhaps*
tamaño (m.) *size*
también *also*
tarde *late*; buenas tardes *good afternoon/evening*
té (m.) *tea*
teatro (m.) *theatre*
televisor (m.) *television set*
tema (m.) *subject*
temer *to fear*
templado *temperate*
temprano *early*
tener *to have*; — que *to have to*
terminar *to finish*
tetera (f.) *tea pot*
tiempo (m.) *time*
tienda (f.) *shop*
Tierra (f.) *Earth*
tímido *shy*
tinto *red (wine)*
tío (m.) *uncle*
tirar *to throw away*
tocar *to play (an instrument)*
todavía *still, yet*
todo *everything*; — recto *straight on*
todos *all*
tomar notas *to take notes*
tono de marcar (m.) *dialling tone*
tonto *fool*
trabajar *to work*
traer *to bring*
tráfico (m.) *traffic*
tranquilidad (f.) *peace*
tranquilo *quiet, relaxed*
trasladar *to take*

tratar *to deal with*
tren (m.) *train*
triste *sad*
trono (m.) *throne*
trozo (m.) *piece*

última vez *last time*
último *last*
universidad (f.) *university*
unos *some, about*

vacaciones (f. pl.) *holiday*
vale *OK*
valer *to cost*
vamos *let's go*
vender *to sell*
ventana (f.) *window*
ver *to see*
verano (m.) *summer*
verdad (f.) *truth*
verde *green*
vestido (m.) *dress*
vez (f.) *time*; de — en cuando *from time to time*; otra — *again*; una — *once*; a veces *sometimes*
viajar *to travel*
viaje (m.) *trip, journey, travel*; — de negocios *business trip*
viajero (m.) *traveller*
viento (m.) *wind*; hace — *it's windy*
vino (m.) *wine*
visado (m.) *visa*
visita (f.) *visit*
vista (f.) *view*
volver *to return, come back*

zapatería (f.) *shoe shop*
zapato (m.) *shoe*
zumo (m.) *juice*

Grammatical index